Film Making in Creative Teaching

Film Making in Creative Teaching

Keith Kennedy

Watson-Guptill Publications   New York

Copyright © Keith Kennedy 1972
First published in the States 1972

Library of Congress Catalog Card Number : 71 114198

ISBN 8230 1745 1

Printed and bound in Great Britain
for the publishers
Watson-Guptill Publications
165 West 46th Street, New York, NY 10036

Contents

Acknowledgment

I am deeply indebted to the many groups of young people with whom I have worked and particularly to the members of the Hornsey group of North London. Many thanks to Christine Allmark, Michael Bevis, David Block, Richard Britton, Douglas Cann, Christine Cope, David Cronk, David Davies, Graham Elliott, Lydia Heller, Steven Holmes, Caroline Neuburg, Keith O'Hagen, David Puddifoot, Rupert Rossi, Linden Salter, Cliff Sarginson, Ann Scott and Teresa Stutz.

I am grateful to the undermentioned film companies for permission to use stills from the following films: Warner Pathe *Camelot*; British Lion *Lord of the Flies* and *Tokyo Olympiad*; MGM *2001: A Space Odyssey*.

I am equally indebted to the following manufacturers for allowing me to reprint photographs of their equipment: Kodak Ltd; Rank Audio; Visual Ltd; Johnsons of Hendon; Sangamo Weston Ltd; Polaroid Ltd; Phillips Electrical Ltd; and Samuelson Film Service Ltd.

I would like to express my gratitude to colleagues Rosalind Claxton, Bob Ferguson, Diane Flower, Janet Hubbard, Roy James, Roy Jones, Humphrey Leadbitter, Charles Peacock and John Quartly.

The help of a number of friends has been invaluable. Christianna Newsholme printed most of the photographs reproduced in the book. Douglas Lowndes and David Reyfield provided photographs of equipment. Mrs Jennifer Malski typed the manuscript. My grateful thanks to all of these.

London   1972   KK

Note to teachers

After a number of years of using film in teaching I have come to the conclusion that although filmstock is obviously necessary in making a film and for carrying out certain kinds of film study exercises, qua simulations of professional techniques, it is equally valuable simply as a *material* for use by groups of students and their teachers. It is as important as paper is as a teaching material. If it once could have been said that education was about bits of paper, now such an assertion can be challenged. Recording devices such as cameras, video tape and sound recorders are tools which, if used, must endow groups with new powers and exciting opportunities to improve systems of communication. The tools, of course, do not guarantee that logical, lucid statements will be produced at the touch of a button. The human factor is too unpredictable for that. Nonetheless, the supply of such equipment to teachers should offer them the chance to think in new terms about new ways of working in their schools and colleges.

Foreword for US readers

The enthusiasm for film courses now evident in universities, colleges, and schools at virtually every level carries with it many tricky problems for teachers and course directors.

Clearly, there is a great deal of muddle and confusion about film-teaching: the relation between 'film history' and 'film-making' is a puzzle; so is the organization and staffing of film courses; so is the matter of equipment, the bewildering variety of hardware, and the range of costs.

It is difficult for an individual school to decide just what approach to take in teaching *Film*. Many schools have leapt into the new activity without sufficient thought of preparation, with the result that student film-makers become frustrated and angry with the school, due to deficiencies in equipment, supplies or organization of the course.

This new British book on student film-making at junior high-school level strikes a calm and reassuring note. The approach is sensible and resourceful, putting emphasis on imagination rather than on expensive hardware. The primary concern is with *film as communication,* not to supplant language but to help develop language, perception, fact-finding, and expression by means of word and picture together.

The author insists that neither language nor film should be an end in itself. Both are tools to help in communication. Students who are perhaps less than literate in language may become highly literate visually; through film they may find a powerful means of communicating their discoveries, sentiments, and imaginative ideas.

The author pays attention to the matter of film-viewing, as opposed to film-making. In music and art, students perform and produce their own work, their own interpretations. In film the same should apply. Film study should not be limited to viewing the classics but should explore the processes whereby the film is actually made; the student becomes a film-maker, not for the sake of making films *per se*, but in order to become familiar with this contemporary means of communication which has so many applications in

other fields: research, documentation, 'note-taking', personal expression, editorial statement.

Film-making by a student group, working together as a group, is of course a social activity. Working outside the classroom on film projects takes the students into the neighborhood, the local community, the city. Immediately, they are working like researchers, investigators, sociologists, explorers, journalists.

In reviewing the equipment needs of a modest film-making programme, much emphasis is given to the use of tape-recorders for interviewing and recording modes of speech. Recorders create a heightened sense of words, of word-use, of expression. Fitting the taped sound to motion picture heightens the sense of correlation between word and picture and sharpens the precise significance of particular images.

For many teachers, there are technical worries and fears in the use of unfamiliar equipment. This study is concerned with dissipating the 'mystique' of motion-pictures and insisting that simple equipment (Super 8mm cameras, stills cameras, simple tape recorders, sound-striping) need present no terrors. Children and teachers can learn their use without difficulty.

The point of view that film is simply a means of expression, a new resource, a tool or device for effective communication, is strongly urged. In this context, it is interesting to consider the ways and means whereby film-making can assist the learning of language. Among many aspects of this process is the possibility of 'seeing' individual words as distinct entities in themselves by filming 'words', by exploring with the film camera such areas as typography, layout, collage, and the printed word associated with other symbols or objects in a visual framework. There is a wealth of stimulus also in the outlines of various school-film projects, all eminently workable and manageable in a school situation. Though the examples are drawn from British schools and communities, and differences exist no doubt in the attitudes and activities of British school children as opposed to American, it is nonetheless easy to draw the parallels and imagine the application of these projects in American schools.

Overall the good sense and sympathy of this study lies in its attention to the resources of film-making as an aid, a stimulus, a new channel for expression and communication. We admit that learning by rote is now archaic; that students often 'turn off' when confronted with didactic teaching; that the teaching of the English language has been bedeviled by many problems; and that clear and exact expression is increasingly difficult to achieve in schools. It is perhaps surprising to consider that film-making as a classroom activity, can assist the teaching of language and communication as effectively as the author claims. Yet when one looks around at the many student films on this continent produced in universities, high schools, and sometimes in elementary schools, the evidence in favor of film-study is highly persuasive.

Given the modest, thoughtful, and resourceful policies outlined here, teachers may well consider that film can be used and taught in a way which will genuinely enrich the learning process. The student stands to gain in heightened powers of perception and expression; he adds a useful skill to his repertory; he tends to become a more thoughtful and committed citizen, seeing his own community with new insight. Perhaps film will become, like language, a basic tool for many literate people concerned with the need for effective communication.

James Beveridge
Director, Program in Film
Faculty of Fine Arts
York University
Toronto, Canada

1   A point of beginning

This book is directed to the teacher who, without experience of film-making or photography, wishes to use film in his teaching. Through the increasingly powerful and fascinating medium of the cinema and television, we are challenged to *see* more completely than ever before. People of all ages are continually having to try to make sense of word and image statements made through these media which aim to educate, entertain, edify, convert or simply to sell something of which we may have little need. We might gain by listening and watching, be educated, converted or even sold a product. But in front of the screen we are at the mercy of the film-maker if we lack the means of construing why he requires our attention in the first place.

The important need is to help all to develop an understanding of the visual media of today as a form of communication : communication between two individuals which must depend not only upon a common understanding of the terms used, but also upon each possessing the appropriate means of expressing them. It is therefore vital to establish standards of visual literacy that will help people to see and understand and respond visually.

This may appear to be the natural job for a film specialist, a new kind of teacher. But there are countless teachers, not film specialists, who find themselves immediately outside the boundaries of the audio-visual aids world, looking hard for a point of entry. Too often they may stand daunted

1   Who are the dockers?

2   Where are buskers to be found?

by the expert, perhaps the college technician or a science teacher, who demonstrates how equipment is to be used with an effortless, but deadly, ease. Deadly, in fact, because the very act of showing how simple it is leaves the onlooker painfully conscious that were his control to fail he would be judged a simpleton. Professional pride, awareness of being about to be revealed to a colleague as a slow learner, will cause many teachers to draw back when faced with the opportunity to use such audio-visual tools as the camera and tape recorder. But it can be easier to say 'I don't know much about tape recorders' than to face being humiliated before one's own pupils by a machine that cannot be persuaded to start.

The choice of a teacher best qualified needs careful consideration. Many teachers of English have accepted the fact that the task of film teaching is theirs. They are moved by a personal interest and the realization that showing films

and making films offers exciting possibilities. Not only should people be able to read picture statements but also they should be able to create them.

It is necessary to stress that any desire upon the part of an individual to communicate his messages or views to another demands that he first identifies to whom he is speaking. In practice, in schools, communication is necessarily a continuum, a constant social interaction between pupils or groups. Every exercise in expression, by using a visual medium, can be seen as a form of social education.

It should not be assumed that the need for the practical study of visual media exists only in the secondary schools among the non-examination classes. It exists equally within those high or grammar schools that may ignore the part that television or the cinema plays in the lives of their pupils.

3 What is marriage?

4 Why do Pakistanis choose to live in England?

2   The use of film in teaching

Filmstock (as distinguished from the finished product of a film) may be used in support of a lesson or course of study where a teacher can involve his pupils in attempts to fulfil exercises by using the camera without working under any obligation to produce a film feature. Given cameras and filmstock, pupils should be able to provide an answer, in image and word, to such questions beginning: Where . . . who . . . what . . . and why, the latter being perhaps the most exciting basis for a project to be undertaken with the camera. There are considerable opportunities for the teacher to employ filmstock in his actual teaching, if it is understood that it is no more nor less than a *material*, and its successful exploitation demands that it be treated as such.

It should not be assumed that written or spoken language is devalued by attempts to speak pictorially; the aim should be to enrich the existing tongue with a host of new words. If, for example, we take the subject of English, we may ask, 'Is a film essay or composition a practical possibility? Can poems and stories be written with the camera? Will the camera assist a pupil in learning words and sentence structures?' Examples of efforts made to use the camera in these ways will be given in the following pages; the proposition to be borne in mind is that filmstock usage in this connection is a means to an end rather than an end in itself. The aesthetic and psychological pressures experienced by the film-maker are not emphasized when film is used

5

6

in this way, though the division made between filmstock usage and film-making is in many ways an arbitrary one. Any camera-user will be confronted by problems of selecting and rejecting, problems of taste.

Some important uses of film in schools and colleges will be discussed in this book, but such a valuable form of teaching as *Film Study* or *The Film Society* will be dealt with only insofar as they relate to the principal argument of the text. The

educational or instructional film cannot be covered adequately in a book of this size, and consequently is not included.

FILM STUDY

What does film study mean? In most schools it designates a combined session of pupils' viewing a film and discussing it afterwards with the teacher

7   In the dockland

8   In the market

9   In the market

10   Not desk based

governing debates. The pupils' attention may be directed either to the subject matter of the film and how it is treated in its context, or to the content of the film as a re-enactment of real events to be compared to the pupils' own experiences and attitudes. The documentary, a film record of real events, may provide yet another sensible talking point between the teacher and his class.

The importance of seeing and discussing films intelligently and clearly cannot be doubted. But the usual policy of excluding the film-making exercise from most film study programmes except on a trial or sample basis deserves to be re-examined. Pupils will profit by being taught how to use the basic tools, no matter how few of them may ultimately become professional film-makers. It is not, after all, demanded of pupils that they become professional writers before they are taught how to write. Where in teaching should the priorities lie? Perhaps the most formative experience for the young is to be had in the actual creating of the flickering images themselves.

THE FILM SOCIETY

In many schools, there are deep divisions in understanding and sympathy between departments, not least between the arts and science factions. If the teachers of the respective departments cannot establish a relationship between their syllabuses, it is unlikely that many pupils will appreciate their interdependence. As an arts-science compromise, any film stands as a major achievement. It is possible for the film society to function as a bridge between the two spheres of knowledge.

The aim is to organize a programme of feature films and shorts that can be shown both to a particular department or group of classes and to the film society. Thus, an afternoon showing of *Billy Liar* to senior English groups might be followed by a general release after school. It might be asked, 'Who in a club would pay to see films with particular relevance to the science subjects?' With the careful checking of catalogues

11   Man and space machine in *2001: A Space Odyssey*

an abundance of material will be found, ranging from the film biographies, *Pasteur, Freud,* etc, to the fantasies of Melies (an opportunity for the physics teacher to discuss the tricks of the camera), to the prognostications of Kubrick's *2001: A Space Odyssey.*

What use, for example, might the history teacher make of such an unhistorical film as *Camelot*? If the history teacher's task is to modify or balance the distorted views of history held by his pupils, a frontal assault can be made by challenging *Camelot*'s handling of historical fact and hypotheses. Of course, many documentary films will be extremely useful to the teacher of this subject.

The following outline of a programme should illustrate how a particular field of study determines the choice of a film which is also of interest to members of a film society.

8 January	Science groups	*Fantastic Voyage*
22 January	History groups	*Billy Budd*
5 February	English groups	*Lord of the Flies*
19 February	Geography groups	*Serenghetti shall not die*
5 March	P E groups	*Tokyo Olympiad*
12 March	Social Studies	*Al Capone*
26 March	Choice by vote by audiences	

There are likely to be some screen educationalists who will object to a film being used rather than presented on its own merits. However, once a large number of films are being shown in his school, the film teacher should not want for examples to create interest in film as art. Such a programme as the one outlined above should demonstrate how the showing of films can become an integral part of school life.

12   Vanessa Redgrave and Richard Harris in *Camelot*
13   A council meeting in *Lord of the Flies*
14   The Russian weightlifter, Zabotinski in *Tokyo Olympiad*

3 Film-making and using film

Once a teacher has been granted equipment and filmstock to use, it is likely that his greatest problem will be the deployment of a class in taking part equally in the actual making of a film. He may have to work with a very large class and make a carefully organized approach in order to involve every pupil.

The group film has been the basis of most film-making exercises in schools. Generally, an effort is made by the teacher to employ pupils in the roles of director and camera crew, in fact, to duplicate the professional unit's roles and to work in their established pattern of shooting script and financial budget.

Such an attempt to make a film with an eye on a professional model means than an effort has to be made to meet conditions customarily encountered when working under commercial pressures. The avoidance of mistakes is vital in the film business, simply because mistakes mean time and a great deal of money wasted. From a teaching point of view, however, mistakes are usually regarded as an inevitable consequence of unfledged effort, to be expected and corrected through demonstration. A pupil's mistakes must happen openly in order that he can be reassured and encouraged to try again. There is, then, an obvious danger in setting up an exercise in which perfection has to be guaranteed before any filmstock can be exposed.

15

16

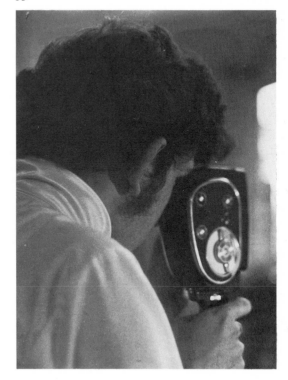

HERE AND NOW: ENVIRONMENT AND SOCIAL LEARNING

The use of filmstock in schools and colleges should not presuppose a concern with subjects that are the preoccupation of the professional companies, but rather with subjects which are the concern of students and pupils, that is, the phenomena of their own world. Many pupils, however, are likely to be entranced by the various make-believe worlds of the screen, and teachers may wish to use film exercises to help the pupil develop an understanding of his own environment and deal with his problems on his own terms. A good starting point might be the school itself as a subject for an exercise.

17 Listening Listening? Sir Idea Attack Innocence

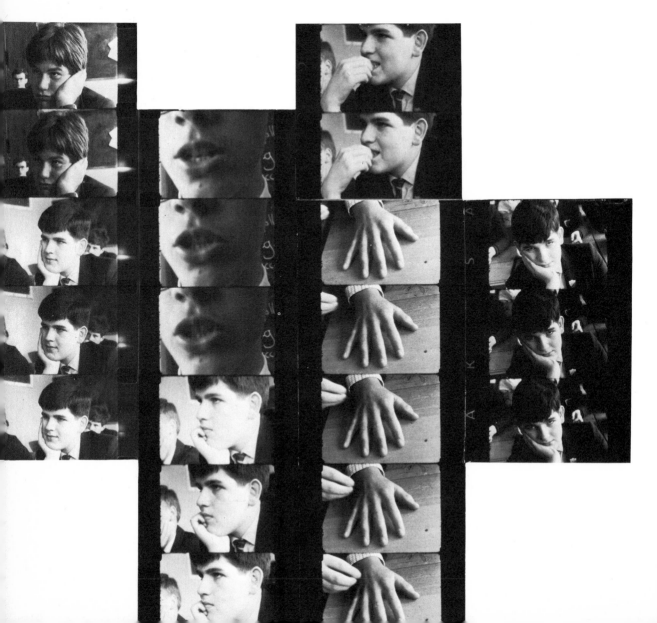

The teacher can use the camera in dealing with the domestic problems of his classroom teaching. He may try to help his pupils appreciate how some problems are likely to arise in any classroom, to institute a form of learning about learning that he may share with his class. The illustrations on page 20, printed from the negative of a 16mm cine film, shot by a group of fifteen-year-olds in a large London school, exemplify this use of filmstock. This was a group film of an unusual kind, each pupil contributing a short script devoted to a particular classroom incident based upon a personal experience, eg

a Hand holding piece of chalk writing on blackboard about Charles II
Sound of boy's voice talking
Hand stops writing, voice stops
Mute, angry face of teacher staring
Hand hurling chalk
Boy clutching eye
b Lips talking rapidly, stops suddenly, slowly tighten
Boy's head lying in folded arms on desk
Grinning faces
Lips talking rapidly, stop, slow smile
Laughing faces
Jerk upwards of sleeper's head
Laughing faces
Sardonic mouth, makes amused comment
Boy's face, looks round room—terrified

The performance of a scene usually involved the participation of the entire group. The camera was operated by successive pairs of pupils for each scene. During the preliminary discussion of the project, it had been agreed that too many films shot by pupils about school life were flights of whimsy, and that too many films produced by adults about schools were sheer exercises in wish-fulfilment. Thus, the group decided to deal with situations familiar to both teacher and class and built a complex of scenes that represented certain real aspects of school life.

In this form of film-making, pupils have a chance to grapple with the problems of their immediate environment. In the film study session, they may be called upon to make comparative judgements between the world of their own experience and the world the cinema presents. But how often does the cinema concern itself with events as they really happen? In a London *Times*

report of an interview with Dr Desmond Morris, author of *The Naked Ape*, the reporter stated:

> The other day Morris was in a bar in Valetta when a fight started between some sailors. 'It was like nothing I'd ever seen in the movies. Screen fights are ritualised, but this was entirely different. There and then I found myself carefully observing human behavior.'

Most film teachers will take pains to offer examples of screen ritual to their pupils, the time-honoured bar-room brawl in the Western, or, perhaps, the comic convention of the antagonism on meeting of the man and woman shortly to fall into each others' arms.

The teacher who is anxious to persuade children to make their own films and thereby create their own standards in the making is likely to want to make absolutely clear what has belonged to Hollywood and elsewhere, and what opportunities face his classes. Earlier in the *Times* interview, Dr Morris had stated:

> I'd like to use film more and more myself . . . Think how useful it would be in studying simple cultural differences. I'd like to set up a camera in an airport, where people of every race are constantly passing through, and just film how they greet each other. We've got to learn how to use our ears and eyes. That's the starting point.

Unfortunately, in most schools and colleges where film is used there may often be a dangerous side effect. The film-maker's use of filmstock endows it too often with a mythic quality, namely, that it is a material that exists primarily for the use of the film artist. Those using cameras and tape-recorders come to regard themselves as film-makers and those without this equipment declare defensively 'We know nothing about it'.

This separation of art and non-art subjects occurs in the face of the fact that filmstock is a material that can be exploited in every branch of academic and non-academic study. In fact, it is the science division that have produced the simplified equipment used by the film-maker. In photography and sound-recording a rapport between the two cultures has been attempted with some success. A pressing need exists for the exploration of the uses of filmstock to teachers of all subjects who feel the need for new materials and methods to extend their teaching abilities.

19   The Gateway Club, Walthamstow, London

THE PERSONAL FILM

The suggestion that a child take personal responsibility for using film in school-time may seem nonsensical at first, neither practically or economically viable. In fact, a small quantity of film-stock can go a long way, and if the aim is for a child to use it as a complementary material to pen, paper and direct experience, it can become an exciting and vital part of a personal project.

The personal film offers the opportunity to the individual to follow his own inclinations. Perhaps only in this kind of film without aim to sell or satisfy pressure groups will be found a freshness and vitality which, even if crudely expressed, will be felt by audiences. In writing of film-making in a grammar school Dennis Russell says

I feel the temptation to help (and thereby to impose one's own view) in the shooting and editing needs to be resisted. Films made by

adolescents are often introverted, almost private, and with little consideration for their audience. But they are likely to be high-spirited and full of bounce and, one hopes, originality. A school film is after all a sophisticated form of child-art; and the lack of polish, the lack of concern for the audience, the lack of self-consciousness, are all part of the charm.

A film can be as personal as the maker wishes. The following photographs were taken on location during the shooting of a short film about a mongol child at The Gateway Club for mentally handicapped children in Walthamstow, London. As a film, it is a personal expression of feeling about the subject by a student film-maker whose younger brother had died of hydroencephalitis several years earlier. His wish to promote the interests of the club and declare his own sense of involvement in the tragedy of mental ill-health were satisfied by making this film.

23

20

21

22

23

24

25

26   Pakistani home in East London

Again, for example, another student film-maker had little knowledge of what it meant to be a coloured immigrant in England. Thus, the film he shot in such locations as a Pakistani home in East London brought him a new experience, and the making of this film was understood to be the means by which he would acquire a personal knowledge of the subject.

While both of the above mentioned examples are forms of documentary, it will probably be accepted by most that a concept of personal film-making inevitably must include the personal fantasy or film made from an entirely subjective point of view.

The films described above were essentially one-man films, conceived and filmed by one person. Nevertheless, assistance was frequently needed and asked for, and anyone asking for help from others automatically committed himself to returning aid when required. The group which is sub-divided into smaller units of personal film-makers will still have to depend upon a degree of fellowship to bind them together in order to share both equipment and experience. This is essential if programming and scheduling is to be effective.

31–33 The subjective point of view

An attempt by the entire class to make a film may present serious problems in finding worthwhile tasks for everyone; nevertheless, there is no reason why, after a year's film-making on a personal basis, a group should not be asked to undertake a production together. The teacher who is prepared to do some detailed programme planning should be able to promote both personal exercise and the group production as an ultimate project.

This book can be regarded as a companion volume to *Film-making in Schools* by Douglas Lowndes (Batsford, London and Watson-Guptill, New York) in which a more detailed discussion of the technical aspects of film-making proper can be found. Teachers will not find they need much help with equipment which, by the manufacturer's definition, is to be operated on a point and shoot basis, but certain fundamental principles should be understood. The major part of these notes are devoted to an elaboration of such data.

An 8mm film-making kit
The aim is to give an outline of the equipment a teacher is likely to find most useful when considering the organizing of either film and tape projects or the making of 8mm films. Where possible, cross-references/have been made to link actual projects described in the text to the relevant technical notes. But, as only an outline has been attempted, a list of books recommended for further reading has been included at the end of this section.

The term *kit* has been employed to describe the equipment necessary to enable the teacher to promote display work and programmes of films successfully, but it should not be assumed that film work cannot proceed unless all the items listed below are available. The camera and the tape-recorder are the key tools and can be used variously in innumerable ways in project work.

The teacher who wishes to promote such projects as a group activity must be ready to work with the simplest equipment available, at least during the introductory stages, in order to forestall possible panic by some of his pupils at being asked to take up 'photography'; he will also be required to be tolerant of poor results at the onset.

The term *8mm* is used in the text with a full consciousness of the emergence of *Super 8* on the market, and the resulting wrangles as to relative merits in terms of picture quality and comparative cost. A brighter, clearer picture is obtained when the latter is projected upon a screen, and as it is enclosed in cassettes, it is easier to load into the camera. However, *Super 8* cameras and filmstock cost more than the standard 8mm equivalent. It should be noted that

if the intention is to start making films tomorrow, 8mm (often referred to as *standard 8*) equipment and filmstock will cost less, but its eventual supercession by the newer gauge is almost certain.

16mm equipment is not discussed in this book, principally because its higher cost and more complex cameras rule out the possibility of it being used *on a daily basis*. However, the chance to launch at least one 16mm project for more advanced students should always be looked for by the teacher.

A description of the principal uses of each part of the film-making kit will be given under separate headings.

Simple stills cameras
The simplest cameras used to take many of the photographs shown in the text are the *Kodak* box cameras. With these cameras, members of a class are able to obey happily the manufacturer's dictum *load, point and shoot* providing their teacher has made a judgement upon the quality, the brightness, of the existing light at the place of shooting, indoors or out. In fact, this is one of the most important tasks he must perform in governing a lesson where cameras are used. The means of assessing the brightness of light is discussed under the heading: *Measuring Light*, page 37.

Cameras of this calibre have fixed focus lenses, which means that every subject will be in focus from approximately five feet to infinity. They possess a small aperture range, *aperture* being the opening behind the lens controlled by a diaphragm by which the light enters, resulting in a sharp definition of considerable areas in front of and behind the principal subject of focus. A small range of aperture means that these cameras can only offer the best results under bright lighting. It is almost certainly holiday-makers' beach photography that has been envisaged by the makers. On dull days, the aperture will not open wide enough to admit the required degree of light.

A further simplification of these cameras has been the recent appearance of the *Instamatic* range, which are cassette loading, meaning the film does not need to be threaded into the camera.

Simple stills cameras were used in the following projects: *Hysteria* page 47, *The Dart* page 48, *The Gun Pit* page 56, *The Playground* page 57, *Alone* page 57, *Barabbas* page 58, *The Tale of a Boy and Girl* page 70, *Stratford* page 113.

34 Simple stills camera: Kodak Brownie Cresta

35 Simple stills camera: Kodak Instamatic 25

The Single lens reflex camera (35mm)

These cameras are likely to be more expensive than those described above, and can be looked to for greater flexibility in focusing under all light conditions, and easier framing of the picture in the viewfinder. The term *reflex* refers to the viewing system which allows the user to look via a mirror-system through the lens itself. Thus, if the user plans to take slides with this camera he can be assured of accurate framing. There is also an extremely wide range of colour and black and white filmstock available for 35mm cameras of various speeds and qualities which box cameras do not have.

36 Single lens reflex camera: Zwiglander Vitoret

37 Single lens reflex camera: Kodak Instamatic Reflex

Unlike the box cameras, greater control can be exercised over aperture size and shutter speeds, which govern the admission of light into the camera. The aperture range of a camera is measured in numbers (prefixed with the letter 'f', standing for factor) often referred to as *stops* f2 f2.8 f4 f5.6 f11 f16 f22, and the higher the number the smaller the size of the aperture. A small aperture facilitates a greater depth of field, which means that by calculation parts of the foreground and background of the principal subject of focus can also be clearly defined. Conversely, by *differential focusing,* a subject before this camera can be shown in sharp focus against a soft or blurred background.

Supplementary lenses can be obtained for the single lens reflex camera (making it possible for the user to focus upon the subject to within several centimetres if he chooses). The normal lens will have a number such as 50mm (5cm) marked on the lens barrel. This number refers to the *focal length* of the lens. The term relates to the angle of view to be had from the point from which the camera is used. Lenses of differing focal lengths can be interchanged at will: the *wide angle* will admit a *wide* vista shot, and the *telephoto* lens will allow the user to photograph a subject in close-up from some distance.

Choice of shutter speed may be made according to whether the subject is moving or stationary. Thus, the photographing of, say, a fight scene may demand a relatively fast shutter speed of 250th of a second, whereas a static subject will require a slower speed of 60th. But, most important, it should be remembered that apart from focusing, variable aperture and shutter action permit the photographer to control the amount of light entering the camera, and thus it becomes possible for him to exercise a greater control in both bright sunlight or dull weather.

Many single lens reflex cameras offer interchangeable lenses, which means the photographer can narrow or widen the field of view if he so chooses.

The following projects were prepared with the single lens reflex camera: *The Photopoem* page 70, *The Photohunt* page 72, *Concepts* page 75, *The Gamblers* page 87, *Birds* page 88, *The Bed* page 99, *The Monastery* page 99, *Up the Junction* page 101, *Patrick Anderson* page 103.

The 8mm camera
Pupils must be able to handle 8mm cine cameras easily and successfully. It is therefore vital to avoid adding the subject of photography to the project in hand, at least in its earliest stages. It is advisable to use the simplest and cheapest cameras at first. These have fixed focus lenses and little or no aperture control. Their range is limited, but it is still possible to carry out practical photography with them. In fact, the use of equipment of this standard can be viewed as a challenge to produce good results within given limitations. (The teacher must be on the alert for signs of 'camera snobbery' amongst pupils who are possibly camera owners themselves.)

At a higher price, cameras can be obtained with the light meter built into the structure which measures the amount of brightness of light and automatically adjusts the aperture to admit more or less light as required. This refinement helps greatly to avoid errors of exposure by pupils.

The viewfinder of a camera enables the user to select the area of the scene or subject to be photographed. In the cheapest cameras these are

38 8mm cine camera: Quartz

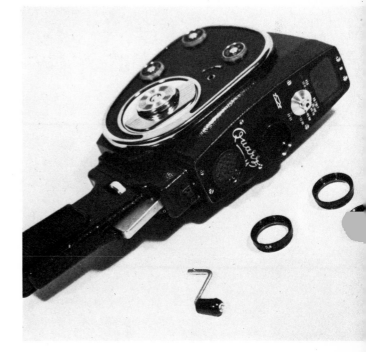

31

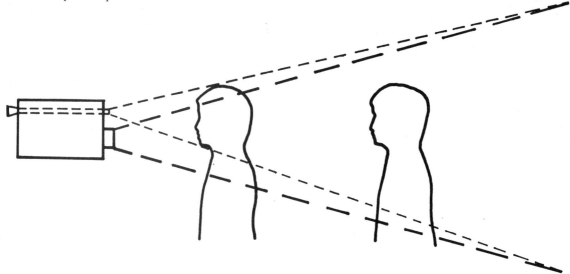

in a different position to the taking lens, and consequently, do not give more than an approximate view of what is about to be photographed. This problem is commonly known as *parallax,* and a correction has to be made after selecting the image area by tilting the camera to align the lens with the subject. More adjustment is needed when working close to the subject (see sketch). However, most children will be able to cope with this difficulty, and many cameras have visible warning signals within the viewfinder that remind the user to make the necessary correction. A reflex viewing system, as described above, eliminates the parallax problem altogether. This refinement means, of course, paying more for the camera. Cameras of a higher price range offer other

40 8mm cine camera: Eumig Superb

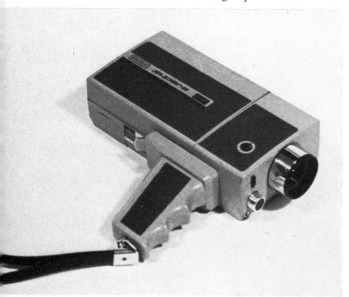

41 8mm cine camera with zoon lens attached

devices that are useful (but not vital) to the film-maker. (It is possible, if looking for an 8mm camera, to buy it more cheaply secondhand.)

Normal filming speed is 16 frames per second for silent films, and 24 frames per second for sound films. Controls for more frames per second are to be found in some cameras. 12 frames per second filming becomes rapid motion (Keystone Cops style) when projected at the normal projection speed of 24 frames per second. If a greater number of frames, 36, 48, or 64, per second are shot the screen action becomes correspondingly slower. It should be noted that change of filming speed must be compensated for by change of aperture: when fewer frames per second are shot less light is required; conversely, more frame exposure per second demands more light. Animation exercises are possible if the camera has a single frame socket to which a cable release can be attached, and one frame exposed at a time (see page 49). In fact, some cameras have a single frame release which is part of the structure itself, but the use of a cable release is recommended in order to avoid shaking the camera.

A rewind mechanism enables the camera user to wind back the film in the camera after an initial exposure without opening the camera, and then expose it again, thus superimposing a second image upon the first. This device is necessary for the film-maker who wishes to use dissolves from one scene to another in his films.

Interchangeable lenses can also be obtained for the more sophisticated cine cameras. These may be mountable upon a *turret*, a revolving disc attached to the front of the camera, or can be screwed into the camera. The long focus, or *telephoto* lens will allow the user to film a subject in close-up from a distance (range is governed by the focal length of the lens). The *wide-angle* lens will enable the cameraman to cover a much wider view of the scene. This lens is particularly useful when filming in a confined space, for example, in a small room where size and structure will not permit the camera to be placed at a distance to allow the entire area to be framed in the view-finder.

A *zoom* lens enables the camera user to vary the focal length of the lens while filming, and he can *zoom* in or move from a wide angle view to a telephoto close-up of detail; for example, from a view of a crowd of people, a movement in to

pinpoint a particular face can be made. This kind of lens offers a greater facility for rapid and easy framing of subject. This is an asset when filming animation or stills sequences by the *rostrum* camera method (see page 49).

A simple non-reflex 8mm camera was used in the following projects: *The Gateway Club* page 23, *The Pakistani Home* page 25, *First Day* page 89.

An 8mm camera with a zoom lens and a reflexing viewing system was used in the following projects: *Animation* page 49, *Once* page 59, *Collage project* page 83, *A Film project* page 48.

42 Improvised method

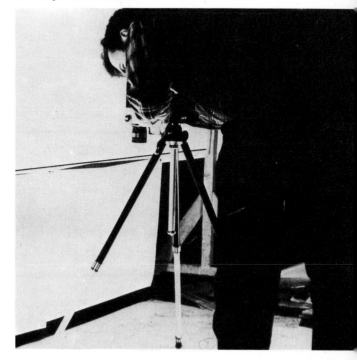

43　Tripod in use

Using the tripod
When the camera-user cannot hold the camera as steadily as he wishes while shooting, he should mount it on a tripod. This tool is a stabilising device, vitally necessary when filming on a rostrum camera basis. Otherwise, each individual film-maker must judge from the results he produces as to his personal ability to hold the camera when filming.

LIGHT: THE TEACHER'S TASK

Most of the camera actions can be learned by rote. The brightness of light can also be measured mechanically, but this task remains one of the most exacting in photography. Thus, the teacher must assume some responsibility for judging whether the available light source is bright enough to make filming possible, what kind of filmstock he can use, and what additional forms of lighting he might employ to ensure correct exposure.

FILMSTOCK

Film sensitivity to light is declared by the manufacturer by a standardised *rating,* denoted by the letters ASA or DIN followed by a number. ASA 400 is a relatively *fast* film suitable for use in limited light; ASA 25 is *slow* and best used in bright light. The faster film has the disadvantage of being likely to lack the high degree of definition and contrast that can be obtained by using film rated at ASA 25 so an attempt should be made to use the latter kind of film where possible. If the teacher wants pupils to be able to photograph subjects of their choice, whether or not the sun is shining, he must be prepared to judge the brightness of the available light carefully, and provide supplementary lighting where necessary. The users of *Super 8* equipment will find that only colour stock is available at the moment with the low rating of ASA 25 for outdoor use, and ASA 40 for use with photoflood lighting. In consequence, the user is faced with a greater task than the teacher using standard 8 equipment, for which a

44　Samcine limpet camera mount used on the side of a car

34

number of filmstocks, colour and black and white, exist, of relatively fast and slow speeds.

It will be necessary to know where filming is to take place, and the probable degree of brightness of light that will be available, before obtaining film. With outdoor filming the element of possible fluctuations in light conditions cannot be eliminated. The teacher can work to a rule of filming at the brightest times of the day (unless, of course, night scenes are to be an integral part of the film). For work indoors, it is necessary to know the size of the room's windows, the colour of the walls and ceiling (light is reflected by these to a greater or lesser degree) and the specifications of the electric light installations. Once the condition of the light, the degree and quality has been determined, the filmstock can be selected according to the appropriate rating. Of course, keeping a supply of filmstock of different ratings is the most desirable method of supporting work in school.

LIGHTING EQUIPMENT

The brilliant, if crude, lighting of a small area is possible by using a quartz-iodine portable light (1000 watt bulb) which can be held by hand and directed onto subject as desired by cameraman. It is also possible to obtain similar lights that clip onto the camera. As heavy shadows are cast by direct lighting, it is better to bounce light from the ceiling, wall or improvise reflectors to achieve a more even lighting. The documentary film-maker will probably accept this form of lighting more readily than those filming a screenplay who may require more subtle lighting. This can be achieved by using photofloods, the bulbs known as: No 1, 250 watts, and No 2, 500 watts in reflectors. These lights can be attached to furniture or fittings by spring clips or placed on telescopic stands. However, in the classroom a battery of lights is not needed to light a simple scene. Thus, a boy and a girl seated at a table can be lit with one 500 watt bulb in a lamp holder. This will result in heavy contrast between the highlit features of the actors and the shadows, but in practical terms such lighting may be most convenient to use; it will serve to black-out the contours of classroom and audience, and allow filming to take place within the hour period of the school.

45   Quartz-iodine portable light

46   Photofloods in use

1 Set speed of film (asa)

2 Hold meter close to subject. When needle stops, take reading of light reflected from subject on scale 1–16

3 Light scale 1–16 repeated on inner ring. Rotate until arrow is in line with appropriate meter reading

4 Select shutter speed and adjust camera aperture to matching f number, eg 125:5·6. Outer scale for shutter speed. Inner scale for size of aperture

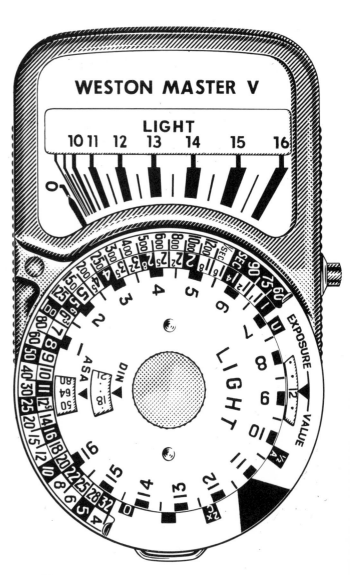

Many cameras have meters that are an integral part of the whole mechanism; the amount of light that enters the camera is governed automatically by this photo-electric cell. Obviously, a teacher attempting to launch film-making in his school must regard this as a boon to his work. However, there are limits to these devices' sensitivity particularly to the range of light being reflected from the whole scene; they make a general reading; it is possible to make a more accurate reading with a meter held in the hand. This kind of meter will measure the amount of light reflected from the subject, the reflected light method, or the amount of light falling upon the subject from the light source, the incident light method. Some meters can measure both incident and reflected light, some will perform only one or the other of these functions. All of these meters possess two scales. After brightness of light has been measured against the first scale (the photo-electric cell causing a needle to move along this side) the reading is checked against a corresponding scale of aperture sizes and the necessary stop selected. The task of achieving correct exposure is vitally important. While automatic meters can be relied upon to a considerable extent, the teacher should learn how to take a meter reading to select the aperture most appropriate to prevailing light conditions.

48

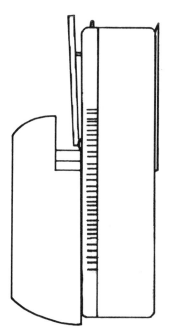

Incident light reading
On Weston meter, cone is inserted
in back window of meter

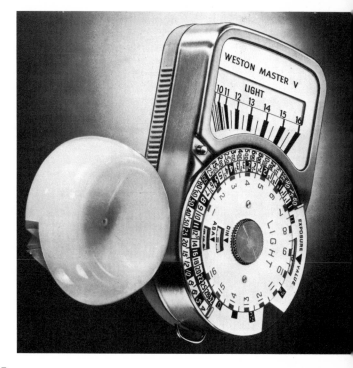

49

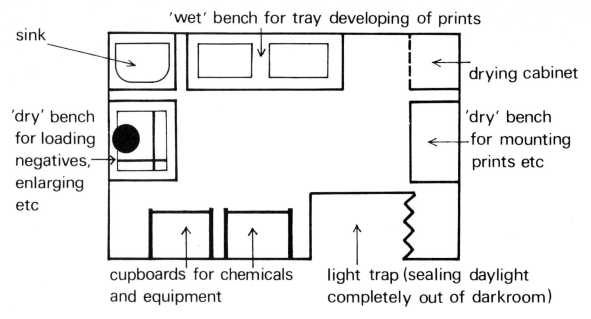

sink

'wet' bench for tray developing of prints

drying cabinet

'dry' bench for loading negatives, enlarging etc

'dry' bench for mounting prints etc

cupboards for chemicals and equipment

light trap (sealing daylight completely out of darkroom)

50   Layout for a dark room

PROCESSING STILLS FILM

Roll film used in stills cameras can be processed by teacher or class in a dark room. Structurally, this unit is, at best, a windowless or 'blacked out' room, with adequate ventilation and a running water supply. The developing and printing of films as a process comprises a number of stages, in which continuity of action is important. Thus, the darkroom equipment must be arranged in such a way to allow the user to work through the stages as smoothly and rapidly as possible. It is a good idea to think of the darkroom as a machine itself, and maintain it as one might look after a specialized piece of equipment. The above figure shows a possible layout, and enumerates the basic stages of the process. It is vital that some arrangement be made other than depending upon the paid service of the local photographic dealer, as this can not be supported by any person or organization for very long. (Note that in the *Polaroid* camera processing takes place internally). The development and printing of coloured photographs is a more elaborate technique than monochrome processing, and most colour film, stills and cine, are sold under a guarantee to

process and return, postage paid. The teacher must make sure that all filmstock used by children can be returned to them in the shortest possible time. Black and white 8mm filmstock is usually sold with processing pre-paid.

EDITING EQUIPMENT

After the return of the 8mm print from the manufacturer, the film-maker faces the task of editing his film. In some instances this can be carried out inside the camera, eg during the shooting of the stills film, or in the animation exercise where the actual shooting can be carefully controlled. Nevertheless, post-shooting editing is really an indispensable process. In fact, one school of thought views it as the point at which the human agent assumes a control over the material not previously commanded during the vagaries of shooting.

8mm viewers are required for a preliminary examination of the returned material. These, in essence, are miniature projectors which allow the film editor or cutter to wind his film *slowly* through the machine, view the film image on a

51 8mm viewer

small screen and control the projection speed by hand. The editor might be concerned with simply removing over-exposed pieces of film, or with creating the film as an artistic entity. The viewer enables the editor to select the pieces of film he wants to join together and to reconsider his choices.

Whatever his purpose, the editor will be required to cut the film, extract the unwanted portions and re-join it. To do this, he will need a splicer, a device which cuts, aligns and cleans the two ends so that a film cement can be applied. After application of the cement, the splicer is locked for several seconds until the film is chemically welded together.

52 Film splicer

THE 8MM PROJECTOR

This projector is a vital part of a film-making kit. The completed film will be projected by this machine. Again, manufacturers' have tried hard to produce machines that are simple to operate. Many are described as *self-loading*, and this means that after starting the projector and introducing the end of the leader into a loading channel the film is drawn automatically through the machine. Many projectors possess a zoom lens which enables the operator to increase the area of picture, although there is a corresponding loss of brightness when this takes place. Several can be bought that possess a *stop-frame* switch, which allows the projector to be stopped on a particular frame, the image *freezing* on the screen. This is useful for discussing work.

Apart from these refinements, perhaps, the crucial issue when considering the purchase of a projector is whether or not the films made are to be given sound tracks or not. Synchronization of projector with tape-recorder can be achieved by a number of methods. The crudest method relies upon marking tape and film and attempting to achieve a synchronized start of both machines from the respective marks. Other devices link tape-recorder and projector mechanically. But, almost certainly, the simplest solution to the problem is for the school to buy a sound projector, which has all the features of the ordinary projector plus a built-in tape-recording device.

Sound on film: After editing, the film must be striped, that is, a thin strip of magnetic recording tape has to be bonded to the unsprocketed edge of the film. Striping can be carried out by a machine designed for this purpose, but it is usually better done commercially. Self-applied striping tends to disintegrate after a short period of time.

Soundtracks can be made by two methods: Sound can be recorded directly onto striped film by using a microphone connected to the input socket of the projector while running the film through the projector. This means that the sound wanted, voice, music, another tape-recording etc will be recorded, but so also will the noise of the projector. Ploys must be devised for masking this unwanted sound. (Some methods for masking sound are described on page 43.) Alternatively, a soundtrack can be prepared on a mains tape-recorder prior to transferring it onto film. This

53 Standard 8mm projector: Eumig Mark 8

54 Dual guage sound projector: Eumig Mark S712D

method makes it possible to use material recorded outside the class-room on portable tape-recorders by transferring it onto the mains tape-recorder. Once the soundtrack is prepared, the output socket of the mains tape-recorder is linked to the recording socket of the projector. As the striped film is run through the projector, the soundtrack is recorded.

There are several points to be checked before buying portable tape-recorders for use by pupils. Are they really portable? And can they be used easily in a slung position while the operator is on the move? The cassette recorders are to be recommended for use with school groups, being light in weight, sturdy and easily operable. The cassette, a plastic box containing the tape pre-set for play when slotted in to the machine, eliminates much of the fumbling and consequent twisting of tapes which can happen when the nervous operator is in a hurry. Many of the models available can be operated either directly from the mains or powered by batteries. These recorders will give the operator the greatest freedom of movement. Once recording is carried out in the street or other places where the noise level cannot be controlled, the operator will need to devise some ploys to help improve the quality of the recording. The four listed here might prove of assistance where the noise level is high:

1   Stand as close to the interviewee as possible,

55   Portable tape recorder with clapper board mounted in position

56   Portable tape recorder: Philips C-60 Compact Cassette
57   Mains (non-portable) tape recorder: Philips 4308

and hold the microphone within a foot of his mouth. *Mask* the noise of traffic by placing your body between the subject and edge of pavement.

2 Buy or improvise a *noise shield* for the microphone. A short *sheath* made from the sponge material used for dish-washing (known commercially in the UK as *Spontex*) will do.

3 Approach your intended subject for interview in a less busy street, or stage your investigations at times when and where mechanical noises are at a minimum.

4 If a commentary by recordist is intended, a *whisper* technique of bringing the microphone close to the mouth and lowering the voice will ensure a better ratio of speech to background noise.

On return to base with these tapes, a transfer can be made of those interviews the recordist considers worth keeping. This means he must connect his portable machine by means of a transfer lead to the input socket of a mains tape-recorder and re-record the chosen material on to a master tape.

THE MAINS (NON-PORTABLE)
TAPE-RECORDER

These machines are not designed to be carried, and therefore it is sensible to move them only when absolutely necessary. To do this will mean less damage to machine or to the person who has to take the strain of moving it. A machine bolted to a bench restricts the chance of it being borrowed or stolen; if movement within the workshop is desired, mounting on a trolley is possible.

In the classroom, a strongly-built machine is needed to withstand the buffetings that can take place in the midst of much activity. Studio performance in the classroom can be best recorded with a mains tape model. A microphone stand will be an asset, but placings following tests of acoustical conditions can be tried. Sound proofing may well have to be improvised in the classroom, especially in those marble-walled, high vaulted rooms of the schools built at the end of the nineteenth century. Some useful materials are cardboard, polystyrene, woollen blankets etc. Alternatively, a large stock cupboard can be easily converted into a mini recording studio.

THE 35MM SLIDE PROJECTOR

Many teachers will be familiar with the kind of projector that possesses a double-slot push-pull carriage which means, regardless of the quality of the projected picture, the teacher makes slow progress when he has a large number of slides to show. The projection of a programme or sequence of slides is best performed with an automatic machine, which allows the operator to load all his slides into the carriage before starting to project. Some models can be operated by a remote control switch, leaving the teacher free to comment upon the pictures he projects. But if commentary or soundtrack is intended, it is possible to project slides on *cues* provided by a tape-recording. The more expensive models equipped with *zoom* lenses enable the projectionist to alter the size of his projected picture.

58   35mm slide projector: Rank Aldis 2000 Auto De Luxe

59   35mm slide projector: Kodak Carousel S-AV

THE LOOP PROJECTOR

The teacher who is looking for the answer to the problem of how to avoid film shot by pupils being shelved after only a few viewings should seriously consider obtaining this kind of projector. Loops of 8mm film can be inserted in cassettes and projected in a matter of seconds with this machine. The loading of the film into the cassette can be difficult, but it costs very little to have this done commercially. This machine is a great asset in display work. The making of 8mm cassettes as teaching aids for other departments of the school can be valuable practice for school film-makers.

60   Loop projector, cassette loading

61   Polaroid camera: Land Camera Automatic 210

THE POLAROID CAMERA

The manufacturers of these cameras guarantee that a print can be produced in 15 seconds. The cheapest, known as *The Swinger,* has automatic light control and a fixed focus lens. In the words of the manufacturers, 'You just aim, shoot and pull a film packet out of the camera'.

Obviously the *Polaroid* has considerable potential for use with pupils. The main drawback is the relatively high cost of *Polaroid* filmstock. But this kind of stills camera would prove most useful to the teacher working with inexperienced groups.

MARKET AND COST FEATURES

Many teachers making the initial effort to use film in teaching will be financially restricted. The possibility of borrowing equipment from friends, staff, pupils etc should be investigated. It should not be forgotten that a great deal of work can be carried out by a group with only one camera.

The teacher should also ascertain what special services may be available to him as a teacher or to his educational establishment. Commercial interests often offer educational discounts on sales of stock and equipment.

It is also useful to know that equipment can be hired, in many cases, at different rates for different periods of time. Also, editing and projection rooms can be hired.

Buying equipment calls for careful shopping. The servicing of equipment is a vital factor to consider. A comprehensive purchase from one source will probably ensure safer service guarantees and also a maximum discount. In buying second-hand equipment it is important to try to obtain some form of guarantee for such purchases.

USING FILM

If the teacher proposes to his class that filmstock is a material equivalent to writing paper, he will commit himself to proving to them that it can be used as simply and effectively as the latter. Of course, short of using *Polaroid* cameras he cannot hope to demonstrate the instantaneous return of a photograph. He is faced with the challenge to bring the members of his group to produce images with the camera as quickly as possible, the proof of the photograph will be in the seeing. Time must not be wasted by talking about films or camera techniques, but put to advantage by using the simplest cameras and the quick results obtained by them.

GETTING USED TO THE CAMERA

The camera is regarded by many people as a kind of talisman, an object supposed to be imbued with magical powers. It is worth ensuring that from the start everyone in the class touches the magical instrument and, best of all, takes a photograph. This can be accomplished quite easily in the classroom or assembly hall. If a hall is used this can be undertaken by seating pupils in a circle with equal spacing between each chair. Next, pre-set the focus of the camera (or use a camera with a fixed focus lens) and ask each pupil in turn to photograph the person on the left (or right). Simple portraiture can be attempted, but it may help to

62–65   Getting used to the camera

provide cues which prompt dramatic responses. The photographs shown above demonstrate a group's reactions to the word *Hysteria* (a dramatic subject being chosen to ensure strong results). In this exercise, each actor performed directly on his cue from the camera user. Then taking the camera in turn he photographed the person on his left. This rotation meant that every person in the group handled the camera. By the predetermination of the distance between each chair the focus of this camera could also be pre-

determined, and only framing in the viewfinder and the pressing of the shutter release button was necessary.

In the above exercise, there was sufficient light to use the camera without any aid other than the use of *fast* film (ASA 400). If this had been a dimly lit interior, it would have been necessary to use artificial lighting. This can be accomplished by holding a portable light behind the camera and directing it at the face of the subject. Alternatively, lights that clip onto the camera are obtainable.

This exercise in camera handling can be achieved in the classroom quite easily. It simply requires evenly spaced desks, a portable light if needed, a camera loaded with film, and subjects.

If the teacher has only one light in a reflector on a stand he may still attempt a variation on this exercise, by having the subjects move in turn into a lit area before the camera. There is some risk in this, however, of losing the spontaneity of the exercise which can help to overcome any resistance by pupils to the fastidious photographer, anxious to produce a perfect print.

Younger children are likely to enjoy dealing with the subject, *The faces I make behind my teacher's back,* and the teacher should have nothing more to do but face the blackboard. The photographs illustrate an exercise of this kind by second-form boys of a secondary modern school, who represented the perils of dart-throwing in the class-room. In this instance, the group depended upon the light entering the room through the large plate windows of one wall and used fast film (ASA 400) and a *Kodak* box camera.

If the simplest equipment is used, and a great effort is made to have the exposed film processed and returned quickly to the children, you might hope for a correspondingly rapid return in interest and a preparedness for more action on the part of your class. Negative developing and printing machines are available commercially, which enables the group to produce photographs within a timespan of 30 minutes. Schools intent on promoting camera work by its classes might seriously consider the purchase of one of these machines.

The event of returning photographs or projecting film to the class is obviously a critical one. Yet, anything less than a responsive reaction should be surprising, given the fact that humans generally evince either a strong desire to see a photograph in which they feature, or an equally strong urge to avoid seeing themselves as revealed by the camera. This situation is open to drawing the group into a discussion of their work and consequently the roles they have adopted in the exercise.

Note The use of a lightweight, portable video-tape-recorder connected with a lightweight television camera and monitor screen adds great

66–68   Using film in the classroom

flexibility and interest to the preparation of dramatized, enacted film projects.

The use of such an electronic unit will enable the film group, during rehearsal, to record a dramatized scene or sequence on tape and play it back immediately to assess the results of acting, direction, and camerawork. There are no delays while waiting for film footage to be processed and returned, and the interest of participating students is fully retained.

Larger schools, having their own television installation for in-school TV production, may be able to offer such a facility for the use of film classes.

Animation
The top of a desk itself can be used as stage for a particular kind of film-making. This is known as *animation*. A teacher at a technical college has written a description of this kind of exercise:

My aim was to involve my class of twelve students in filming an animation exercise during an afternoon period, using the *rostrum* camera method. By this method the camera is mounted on a stand or tripod and pointed diagonally or vertically at a board on which cut-out figures can be moved, or drawings or stills placed. During filming the camera does not move except for the possibility of *panning* or *tilting* across the face of a photograph or a drawing if either of these are large enough to accommodate such actions. The board has to be illuminated by two photoflood lamps, 250 watts each, each placed at an angle of 45°. (See drawing.)

Arriving before my class, my first step was to pin a 1220mm × 915mm sheet of white paper on the floor; erect a tripod before this, and place the lamps on the opposite side of the sheet of paper, after connecting them to the main power source with the help of an extension lead.

Next, I loaded the 8mm camera with a roll of *Kodachrome*, film LI Type A (indoors). This camera possesses a reflex viewing system, a zoom lens, and an automatic light-measuring meter. The reflex viewer and the zoom lens are a vital need in this form of filming. After screwing the camera to the tripod head, I inverted the camera, pointing the lens down to

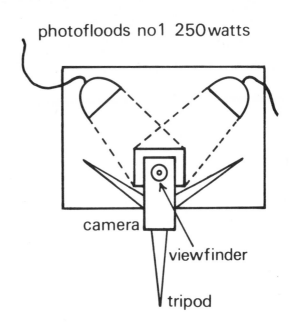

photofloods no1 250 watts

camera

viewfinder

tripod

69 Animation exercise   Camera set-up

the sheet of paper and secured it in this position by tightening the screws. The camera was now ready for use.

I stationed a table between the students' chairs, arranged in a semi-circle, and the camera and placed a pile of magazines and drawing paper, scissors and felt-tip pens on it. I was now ready to introduce the subject to my group:

Men and Women

On arrival I invited my class members to work individually in selecting pictures from the magazines which depicted men and women in everyday situations, and to decide what possibly one might be saying to, or about, the other. My group comprised boys and girls in equal measure, and, of course, I recognized that the exercise gave plenty of scope for vengeful or ribald comment.

Thus after the selection of a picture, the imagined comment was displayed by cutting out *a speech balloon* from the paper provided, writing in the words, and placing it close to the lips of the chosen *speaker*.

Each statement was filmed in a boy-girl-boy rotation in the following manner. The picture was placed under the lens of the camera and 8 frames of film exposed. Next, the *balloon* was added to the picture and filmed with the length of the exposure being governed by the time taken to read the statement through the view-finder eyepiece. Finally, the *balloon* was removed and another 8 frames of film exposed. Eventually, when the finished film is projected these balloons appear to leap from the lips of the figures in the pictures. The final result was, in fact, a cross-bombardment of denunciation and denigration. Nevertheless, a debate had been launched.

This part of the exercise lasted for an hour, and the second stage of the session was given to the actual process of animating cut-out figures, men and women, under the theme of *The Battle of the Sexes*.

Firstly, to demonstrate what was to be attempted. On projecting the finished film the cut-out head and shoulders of a woman can be seen to be shaken and then she places her cheek against the shoulder of a male beside her. To accomplish this it was necessary to lay the cut-outs under the camera; to film them for only 6 frames (using a cable release attached to the single shutter release socket in the camera) and then, after stopping the camera, to move the female figure closer to the male, but only fractionally, and to film again exposing exactly the same number of frames as before. This procedure was carried out unvaryingly until the woman's cheek rests on his shoulder.

On projection of the film after processing, the images appear to move together under their own volition—they have been animated.

Every pupil used the camera in order to film his own action sequence. All had worked hard and vented much feeling about the sex opposite to his or her own, but it required more than the allotted three hours to complete this exercise. When it is noted that approximately 4000 frames, each a single photograph, were exposed it becomes easy to understand why.

The classroom equipped for everyday teaching can only be regarded as a one-set studio. Films about classroom situations, of course, can be easily staged. Other settings required, eg a café, a living room or office, might be best contrived in a corner of the room cleared of school furniture. A group intent upon staging an incident in a café needed a table covered with a cloth, cutlery and pre-cooked food, and set these in a corner of the room decorated with travel posters. Carefully chosen angles of shooting and restricted lighting helped to convey the atmosphere of a café. Limiting light to the use of one bright source can prove sufficient to film interiors one might expect to be dimly lit, eg bedrooms, prison cells etc. For another group the use of an armchair, a reading lamp, a victim, scissors and tomato sauce —lots of it—were the sole properties necessary to enact a bloody scene before the camera within the hour period on their timetable.

70–74   Rehearsal and Performance

The script

Once a willingness to handle the camera has been established, the question of choice of subject becomes relevant. Does every subject chosen to be photographed have to be worked out on paper? This is a decision to be made by the individual or group in considering each task that confronts them. It seems a natural opportunity for the teacher to set a writing exercise, but the danger is that finally there will be a script, but no film. If a treatment, the outline of a story with technical notes about intended filming effects, or script, will solve such problems as when and where shooting is to take place, and what is needed from actors and the props man, then it is recognizably a practical measure. But if the script-writing becomes a substitute for the film-making itself then time and energy has been wasted.

What is a script anyway? One contemporary director considers it to be 'sheets of notes for those who at the camera will write the film themselves'. Jean Luc Godard finally produced a copy of his script for *Alphaville* only after the film had been shot and edited. A script can be as much or as little as you need in order to progress in the making of your film.

It may be as short as this:

The end

1   A close-up of an alarm clock—after one minute it explodes.
2   Another alarm clock is seen—after two minutes it explodes.
3   A third alarm clock is seen—after four minutes a hammer held by a hand smashes it.

Michael Bevis, art student

A poem may become the script:

After the bomb

Fire and flesh,
   hails down like a winter storm,
Foul, smelly gas erupts, seeping into our bones,
The little life that is left,
   follows a distorted pattern beyond logic,
Time is now a dimension left out,
and emptiness takes over.

Destruction; disintegration never diminishes,
   and positive action has now only negative
     results,
Gone are the senses to feel emotion and pain,
And everything is silent amongst the abundance
   of sounds,
Blackness now follows that light,
That was the beginning and now the end,
And death is an addictive drug.

Michael Bevis

The filming was carried out entirely by the writer, using a number of his own paintings, magazine cut-outs, and long, slow *panning* shots of houses being demolished on a derelict housing site. The sound track embodied the reading of this poem to electronic music performed by his friends.

In this form of scripting, the film-maker's aim was to work alone and thereby control the exercise very carefully himself. He hoped that in his hands the film would develop a rhythm and a logic that could not have been achieved by attempting to follow the *fait accompli* of a script. Making the film became as personal an act as the writing of the poem.

Yet, the carefully prepared script may give the film-maker a foundation which frees him from being over-taxed by detail. Film director, Robert Bresson, explains in an interview, 'it is necessary to have a base, a solid base, for one to be able to modify a thing, it is necessary, at the start, that things are very clear and very strong'. But later, in the same interview, he adds, 'I have done the best of what I have done when I found myself resolving with the camera difficulties that I had not been able to overcome on paper'.

Thus, a script is likely to be as detailed or as simple as the film-maker requires. It may be as carefully organised as this:

Lost (extract)

Location A The north side of Blackfriars Bridge, towards nightfall.
1 *Pan* around tops of mushroom-shaped lights at underpass, left to right, facing river. Slowly and deliberately.
2 *Fixed shot* of the underpass, from the same position as (1) with the camera at a lower angle, facing down the embankment.
3 *Fixed shot* of a figure standing forlornly silhouetted against the sky, at the point where the pavement runs onto the bridge.
4 *Close-up* of the same figure—head and shoulders—against a plain background. *Studio* —the figure is first seen with its head bowed, facing slightly to one side. Slowly it raises its head and looks towards the camera.
5 *Pan* from the end of Blackfriars Bridge (camera position), first looking up New Bridge Street, held firm for a few moments, then the camera moves round slowly (left to right), halting as it looks up Queen Victoria Street, then round again past the Underground Station to the railway bridge and finally coming to a halt as it looks across the bridge.

Sound

Location A to allow the tape to start before the film, the first sound unit should begin before 1, and end just before 3. The music consists simply of Beethoven's Piano Sonata, Op 14, No 2; only the opening arpeggios are heard. At about the end of 2, a male voice begins to speak, neither flatly nor emotionally:

'I was lost, utterly lost in this bizarre city. The things around me were not me, and I could not tell or feel what they meant. Everything was passing me by.'

During 5 the voice continues:

'What mind could have imagined these heartless, soulless shapes? And what mind from among them could understand me?'

The seventeen year old writer-director of this script lost interest in the film after several days shooting, and the film has never been completed. Writing for the screen can sometimes become a vicarious satisfaction, with the writer avoiding a further commitment by proceeding with the filming. However, the writer who does make a film from his script may realise a richer reward. The Soviet director, Sergei Gerasimov has said, 'Writing a script gives me a great satisfaction, sometimes more than directing the film. You see the ideal film when you're writing, but it's very hard to realise this ideal when you actually shoot because it depends upon circumstances you can't control, how good the cameraman is, for instance. On the other hand, you may hit on things which enrich your original conception. That's one of the delights of film-making'.

Another useful method of script notation is to draw the visualized scene or shot (as carefully or crudely as you wish) in a sequence. This is usually described as the *story board* method. It is possible to prepare an outline of a story or play by attempting to photograph intended dramatic climaxes or significant detail in advance. The opportunity to make statements in visual terms may result in success after a failure with words. The teacher should watch for such chances to allow a pupil, suffering from mental blocks about writing, to find and use this alternative method of communication. Success in one medium may dispose the pupil to try again in another, and if the teacher can offset failure by encouraging the pupil to use a picture language, he may come to use words (without resentment) later.

The writing of a script can too easily become the basis of a lesson; it should be remembered that a script is generally used as the foundation of an activity and not a substitute for it. If the making of a film is the stipulated aim, the film is all that should matter.

① DRRRING. 5A.

② O.K. SIT DOWN

③ COX + BRADY — STOP TALKING!

④ WHO? ME SIR?

⑤ YES — YOU BRADY

⑥ I WASNT TALKING.. (SARCASTICALLY).. SIR!

⑦ COME HERE BRADY!

⑧ GET LOST.

⑨ STAND UP BOY!

⑩ ALRIGHT, SIR —

⑪ ER... SIT DOWN BRADY.

USING FILM IN SCHOOL OR COLLEGE GROUNDS

'I am sure that some teachers have been drawn to screen education work because it offers them a freedom they do not have within their own specialist subjects'

H R Wills, Screen Education

Outside the school building the playground or playing field can be regarded as an extension of the studio stage used indoors. The exercises described below are examples of this *al fresco* work in which the participants were asked to develop a storyline or action sequence from a given subject in an area within the boundaries of the school or college premises.

In *The Gun Pit* exercise the consequences of a direct hit by a bomb were worked out, photograph by photograph, by three fourteen-year-olds in the corner of a playing field of a London secondary modern school. One roll of film was used in a *Kodak* box camera, and they provided their own stage properties.

76–81   The Gun Pit

The following lesson carried out by a class of fourteen-year-olds, from a secondary modern school, was organised in the following manner:

24 children—6 groups of 4—one box camera and a roll of film to each group.

Theme *The Playground*

Procedure each group will take a sequence of photographs that will tell the story of an event that either actually occurred or might have happened in the playground.

Possible subjects The Fight, Sweets, The Accident, The Quarrel, The Missing Pen, Tag, Cigarettes

The aim of this exercise was declared as an attempt to lead children to discover that a story develops logically, has a framework of varying dramatic incident, and can be worked out to a climax. Almost every child knows this (television, cinema and comics inform him) but many have difficulty in telling stories *in words*. Many children (especially those of the secondary modern) if compelled to use words in writing and speaking, are humiliated; their inadequate word supply has to struggle to satisfy their own highly developed sense of dramatic story. Thus, in this exercise the children used simple cameras to tell stories in visual images, and created these stories together.

The pleasures and problems of living alone were discussed by a class of eighteen-year-olds training to be child welfare nurses, and then they took to different parts of their college to try to portray aspects of isolation before the camera.

82   The Missing Pen

83–84   Project on Isolation

The Biblical figure of Barabbas was used as a subject for a second form exercise in which the thirteen-year-old boys re-enacted the story as a play, embellishing it as they saw fit with lots of violent action. Then, they took their play onto the school playing field to be filmed. As the field looked out on the surrounding industrial suburb, there were difficulties with backgrounds and sky-lines. These were solved by sharply angling the camera so that the subject was framed either against the sky or ground, or, again, by masking the unwanted factories and houses from sight by grouping the actors before them. Later, the photographs were enlarged by two of the group's teachers and these were filmed, using the *rostrum* camera method.

85–87 Barabbas

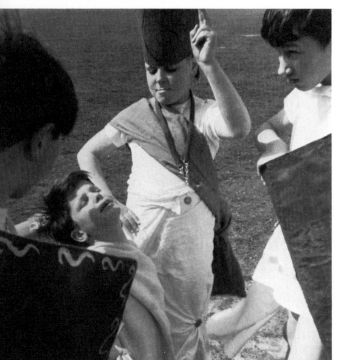

The exercises described above were carried out in school time, usually within the hour-long period. Nevertheless, results were obtained which were sufficient to provide a foundation for further written work and class discussion. While the making of a film was rarely mentioned, on seeing their results, pupils would ask quite often if they could make a film. By the method of film-making referred to above, namely the rostrum camera, it is always possible to extend an exercise. As an example of this, a study of student sunbathers carried out by fellow students progressed by degrees to become the story of a quarrel between a girl and her boyfriend who possessed a roving eye. A cine camera was used to film the quarrel between the pair and the enlarged photographs filmed in the studio. The edited result was a short film, the sum of two different enterprises.

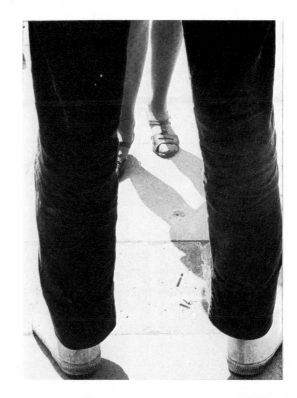

88–90   The Quarrel

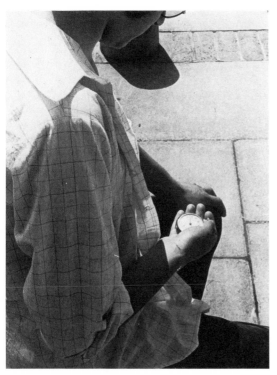

The greatest obstacle to any teacher leading out his pupils into the street whenever he wishes is the opposition of most educational authorities. It is outside the scope of this book to discuss fully such a complex educational problem, which centres upon the unbending attitudes and cowardice of education authorities, boards of governors, and teachers. Fear of their pupils moving before the public's eye and attracting undue notice governs many headmasters' thinking about how open their schools should be. But one factor should be pinpointed: the teacher is without the right to say 'yes' even to the senior child who wishes to make an unaccompanied trip into the street. The parent possesses this right beyond question, and, above a certain age, son and daughter are the fetchers and carriers for the household. The risk of accident is ever-present, but at a family level the risk is usually admitted and taken. With pupils eleven to sixteen years of age, it is the particular responsibility of the teacher to advance their understanding of the society in which they live. He needs the right to sanction the comings and goings of pupils, in order that they may 'fetch' and 'carry' information and experience into the school. The risk of accident exists, (as it must for the child running errands or packed off to the afternoon cinema by distracted parents during the school holidays). But if the teacher is a good teacher then he is probably an ambitious person. The ambition might be no less than the wish to involve the pupil in constructive and interesting work which is not always achieved in the classroom.

School milk isn't everything

During a discussion with a group of fifteen-year-olds on the problems of 'enjoying school in your final year', it was suggested by one boy that we adjourn to the local café for our mid-morning break. I suggested that milk was available at the school and was very nourishing, and received the crushing reply that milk wasn't everything. So we crept out of school, the boys leading the way through a back lane, and spent our hour in a local transport café, where our conversation continued in a relaxed manner.

Two boys who visited Billingsgate, the London fish market, with a tape-recorder and a camera, found a café the most convenient place for meeting people who had time to talk to them:

KELVIN (reading into the microphone from *A Guide to Cafés* written by Jonathan Routh) Joe's No 1 Snack bar, 1 Lower Thames Street. This simple white-tiled place frequented by simple, foul-mouthed, white-coated fisherfolk from Billingsgate, is a real find, run by Joe and Edna. It appears to be a part of the adjacent church of St Magnus the Martyr, and the text in the window says 'our Motto is cleanliness and civility' ... What do you think of that description?

EDNA Very true, at times. They are foul-mouthed.

KELVIN What about simple?

EDNA Oh, on their own side. Very simple.

JOE They've got a language of their own.

But later the boys after speaking to a number of the 'fisherfolk' were able to decide for themselves:

KEITH What exactly do you do?

PORTER Portering, fish portering. Carrying boxes of fish from the shops and vans to the vans that deliver them out of London. In all winds and weathers you know, we've seen some winters down here. Snow up to your ankle and slush up to your knees and raining so much you've got to change three or four times a day, but I still wouldn't be out of the market.

KEITH What are your hours?

PORTER We actually start work at 6.00 am—finish about 11.30 am. I reckon my starting time is the time I get up, 3.30 am, and I come out at 4.00 am.

KEITH Every morning?

PORTER Every morning. Thirty-seven years. Except for the war years when I was away of course. I would say this is the life for anybody, nobody leaves the market you know, once they belong to it.

In markets people can be found who regard talking to the public as part and parcel of their business. If teachers regard this question-and-answers sort of interchange as a sensible practice for their pupils, such places as markets are well worth visiting.

91–93 Billingsgate

A group of students who decided to make a study of the reasons why Americans visit this country found themselves involved in talking for hours to people who were feeling isolated as strangers and longing to talk to 'real' English people. These Americans' gratitude was often expressed by offers to buy refreshments and invitations to join them in 'doing the town'. But while their hospitality was being sampled, discussion in depth upon such topics as Vietnam, civil rights and scores of issues took place. The subsequent linking of transcribed statements from the tape-recordings with photographs of the speakers proved an effective form of presenting the collected information to other pupils.

94–95   Project on Tourists

'Film . . . is uniquely equipped to record and reveal physical reality and, hence, gravitates towards it'

Theory of Film   Siegfried Kracauer

This exercise calls upon young people to visit locations unknown to themselves, that is the *adventuring,* and to return with film and tape-recordings of their visits. At the onset, special demand for information is made in order to have them focus their attention upon a particular aspect of the given area. Talking to people is an essential part of the exercise, in light of the group's aim to learn as much as possible about the people they meet and the places observed. There is a challenge written into the exercise to use the cameras and tape-recorders they carry to record the significant movements and minutiae witnessed in the area they are visiting. A typical guide sheet looks like this:

96

Your work area is   *Covent Garden*
Bus No *29* will take you to *Bloomsbury Square*
Can the area you are visiting be said to have 'a definite character' of its own? Use your cameras and tape-recorders to record your findings.

Consider the following questions:
What are the qualities of structure, colour, texture, sounds and smells that give a particular area its own identity?
Who are the people (definable by the camera and tape-recorder through their visible social and personal characteristics) using this area?
Should you begin by recording the obvious?

After you have finished filming you must make your way to Trafalgar Square (within walking distance of the area in which you are working). Try to arrive at 12.30 pm and wait by the seats nearest to South Africa House. 1.00 pm is the latest at which equipment should be returned to this point.

97

It is possible to divide your class into small groups and assign them to work in adjacent areas. Thus a re-assembly can be made at a point central to these areas. An element of surprise can be introduced in these ventures by sending out groups under sealed orders. This means that only as a group boards a bus or train is it given its guide sheet and details of destination.

The emphasis has been laid upon *place* in the above exercise, but it is just as easy to consider *people* as the subject. Usually, it surprises and delights young people to discover that most adults will find the time to stop and talk to them, and, moreover, that most have a tale to tell (examine the interviews printed further on in the book for evidence of this).

98–102

103–107

The following 'adventure' called upon the participants to approach passers-by with tact and courtesy and carry out a conversation:

CAMERA ADVENTURE

Here and now

The Interviewers
It is Sunday morning. The time is probably between 10 and 12 pm. You are going to meet and talk with people in the streets of an East London area. They may be local residents or visitors.
Draw their attention to the surrounding conditions of the street; people; time and weather. What are their feelings (feelings: 'consciousness of pleasure or pain . . . opinion as resulting from emotion', Chambers Dictionary) about these?
Your real subject is the interviewees themselves. The declaration of this to the subject would probably be difficult to make and might stilt conversation. Questions must be devised with care. Base your questions upon the present, ask for opinions of what can be seen, *take your cues from what can be seen*. The cameraman will depend upon these cues as his task is to photograph what is happening and must be guided by references made by the interviewee to the surrounding scene. Focus your questions upon *the here and now*.

Cameramen
Should take their cues from the statements made by the interviewees. Photograph both the subjects and the aspects of the scene to which they refer.

The cine camera should not be used for the collection of random shots. This is the function of the stills camera. It is likely that certain references to the street scene can be developed as a theme. For example, if a number of your interviewees refer to a local traffic problem, let *Traffic* be your theme and base your film upon this subject.

Group No . . . will travel by bus No . . . to . . . and proceed to . . . Re-assembly point is outside the Whitechapel Gallery (near Aldgate tube station) *at 12 pm.*

108   'I came to England after I left the Israeli army . . .'

109   'In Calcutta, I was a police magistrate there . . .'

66

110 'I'm going back to Dublin tonight—will you send me a photo?'

111 'I found myself starving on the Thames Embankment seats and one of them has got my initials on it . . .'

112 Question: 'Are you married?' Answer: 'I'm a seaman.'

113 'I went completely blind and God healed me and that's why I'm a Christian.'

114 'Happy? When I'm fishing . . . we'll be here all night.'

115 'I'm happy when I'm with my boyfriend.'
116 'Happy? I don't know . . .'
117 Why do so many models advertising clothes strike laughing poses?

What is laughter

Similar uses for the tape-recorder and camera can be found valuable in the more formal project. A group of students were asked to study the phenomenon of human laughter. They began by pairing off in observation patrols to watch people laughing in the street:

At the top of the escalator a girl got her heel stuck in the grid. She laughed in an embarrassed way along with the girl with her. A man with a moustache laughed at something the ticket collector said. His moustache curled up at the corners. A group of boys were larking about. When a friend arrived one of them stuck his foot out and the friend laughed sarcastically. You could hear him laugh, but without facial movements.

This extract is from a report written a short time after watching these people. The project was developed further, with the students being asked to gather as much visual material concerned with laughter as possible. Sound-recordings of both laughter and stimuli, jokes, rhymes and accounts of amusing experiences were collected. Finally, several camera adventure exercises concluded the group's enquiries:

1 *Laughter*
Consider these questions:
Can you recognise that a person is feeling happy. Does happiness show?
Is laughter usually an indication that a person is happy?
If not, what kind of laughter might it be, eg derisive laughter, a hollow laugh.
How you had a good laugh lately?
Are you feeling happy at this very moment?
Put these questions to those people you meet and record their answers.

2 *Happiness is . . .*

Today, at this moment, are you happy? Who can describe what it means to be happy? Have there been times, moments, hours, days, months, years, in your life during which you were happy?

What possibly are the tokens of happiness that you might recognise, today, in the street as you talk to people and observe their behaviour?

The questions you ask should create opportunities for your interviewees to describe their state of being, happy or unhappy as it might be. Please photograph your interviewees in close-up, but pay attention to focusing!

Exercises of this nature can involve young people in listening to and observing people who are often older and have experienced more than themselves. The experiences they relate frequently consist of the stuff that drama is made of. The school or college anxious to develop its own film-making and drama activities should not miss the significance of this, but should look beyond the social studies aspect of this work to the possibilities of literary or creative work by pupils based upon the collected material. Film material can certainly be incorporated in stage and film settings in a number of ways. These will be discussed later.

In fact, there is no reason why literary exercises should not begin by enlisting people in the street. For example, the members of one group were asked to question people in the street about dreaming, to photograph dream phenomena and later to relate these images to texts written by themselves.

The participants in this form of exercise can be despatched to an unfamiliar location and asked to make up a story on the spot, the camera and tape-recorder providing the means by which the created story returns to base with the group.

118 Jesus wept—but in the gospel there is no reference to him laughing. What kind of men live without laughing?

119–120 Dream reconstruction

This means that creating a film sketch, photo-sequence or photo-poem is the principal task. For example, the following limitations were imposed upon groups who were directed without advance knowledge to Epping Forest:

The Tale of a Boy and a Girl
This story must be devised on location in pictures recorded by your cine cameras and words spoken into your tape-recorders.

To begin with your story must follow a set pattern; the following headings outline this. It is your task to interpret these headings:

a Dejection
b A Glimpse of HER
c Following
d The Encounter
You must develop the story from this point

All were advised to decide what was to happen in their stories and attempt a pre-allocation of film footage for each sequence. Each was allowed one roll of black and white film, and the cameras used had fixed focus

THE PHOTOPOEM

For another group the demand to create a photopoem was understood as a call to 'create on the move'. The directions: choose your visual image and record it with your camera; now record a statement on tape. At the end of the exercise you should have a series of visual images that share a relationship with your recorded statements. Later you will have to complete this poem. An example of this exercise is shown below:

Think of
a time
that you remember well
a time
when you
were part of feeling
(watch the child and you will remember)
pretend nothing:
feel again
and
look at us,
see us as symbols of feeling
and
laugh at us—it is all you can do.

Christine Allmark

121–122 The Tale of a Boy and Girl

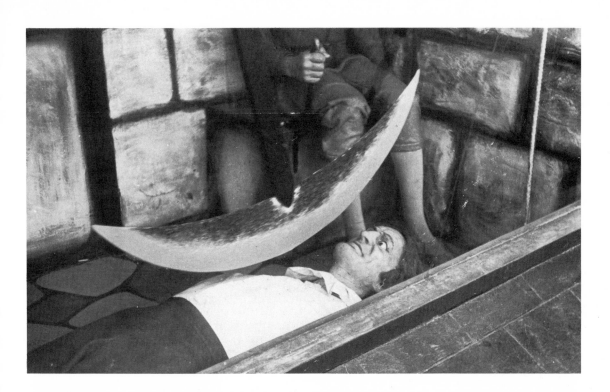

123–124   The Photopoem

This exercise calls upon the members of a group to carry out a search for a number of articles or living subjects, photograph them, and then invent a narrative embodying each found subject and object. After the making of the story, the exercise can be continued in another direction. For example:

A photohunt and improvisation
Location Wood Green High Street and adjoining streets.
Part 1 Locate or invent the following subjects and photograph them carefully:
   1   A bottle standing upon a doorstep or window ledge
   2   An eye catching poster
   3   A young couple courting in a public place
   4   An old lady carrying a shopping bag
   5   A pair of shoes resting upon the edge of a kerb in a busy thoroughfare
   6   A young man or woman telephoning from a booth with the door open
   7   An employee of the local council performing a public duty
   8   A sleeping figure
Part 2 On your return to the centre you will create a short play embodying the above subjects. Stage properties will be available for this.
The tape-recorder During your search you should begin the working out of your story line, and you have been given a tape-recorder to assist you with this.
You must record a conversation with *a* The old lady you photograph *b* the council employee. The topic to be discussed with these people should relate directly to the theme of your play.
All groups must return by 4.30 pm at the latest.

The exercises described above are only some of the ploys that might be used to bring your pupils into contact with the world outside the school. The further development of such work can only depend upon the needs of the pupils concerned and the teachers' own aims and abilities. Although much of the work described can be seen to have a social studies or literary bias, the accent could have been placed as easily upon historical or scientific enquiry without the loss of the intrin-

sic value of making personal contact with other people.

125

126

127–133 The Photohunt

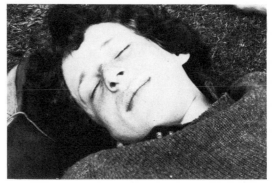

4   Film and English

'. . . if language is only one medium among many into which thinking can be translated, then the importance of 'literacy' in its traditional sense, would need to be reconsidered.'

Language: Some Suggestions for Teachers of English and Others, 1955

It seems obvious, today, that thinking can be translated into media other than language. A child is likely to be able to compose an essay upon the hoary old subject of *A Walk in the Countryside* as easily with a camera and tape-recorder as with pen and paper. Perhaps the camera can describe the ordinary, simple objects that surround us more successfully than an attempt made by a person with words. In terms of aesthetic appreciation, a more immediate response to a subject might be made by the pupil if he is able to record what his eye sees with a camera. The prospect of visual literacy (to be able to see and understand) becoming a co-ordinate of verbal literacy (to be able to read and write) is a real one now because of rapid developments made in equipment manufacture and increased public interest in the media of the visual arts. The teacher of English may seize the opportunity to open the eyes of his pupils to a medium that employs *both* vision and sound, image and word.

Candidates for a General Certificate of Education, Ordinary level English paper* were asked to choose these subjects for composition:

a   Man's relationship with animals
b   Describe a scene of people at work

Would many youngsters have difficulty in finding material examples of these subjects in the streets outside the school and recording them with a camera? I believe they would not.

A more difficult choice might have been:

c   Describe a district or country you have

visited which is quite different from the place where you live.

To attempt an answer to this question with a camera would necessitate making a journey by choice to a known, or unknown place. But this might prove to be a more formative and exciting experience than writing an account of a place remembered, regardless of the pleasure of indulging in memory exercises.

How might a pupil compose an answer to this question on film or tape:

d   What invention or discovery of the last hundred years has made the greatest difference to man's life? Give reasons for your choice.

The acquisition of visual information about the inventions and discoveries of the last hundred years would probably take a long time. But the question relates to 'man', who, of course, is available in abundance and variety both within and outside the school, as potential subject for tape or film. The pupil might well be asked to reveal knowledge of human beings, apart from supplying information about invention or discovery, and the camera and tape-recorder can help him to do this.

Nevertheless, the teacher may hesitate, thinking such work is for the art or film specialist. But there are important reasons why the teacher of English should consider using the camera and portable tape-recorder in his teaching.

Training a child how to use a language is an attempt to equip him for the formidable task of dealing with other human beings. Any teacher seeking to fulfil this aim will find the world full of ready made teaching aids: people. He would be well advised to enlist their help. His pupils can be brought out of the classroom to meet and talk with other people: from the casual encounter in the street to the confrontation with an authority who claims special knowledge of a subject; to the observing and recording of experiences with camera and tape-recorder. If filmstock is taken to reveal physical reality, then the teacher should

* In the US this would be the equivalent of the examinations taken by high school seniors for their high school diploma.

allow his pupils to use this important material to gather substance for study.

Making a comparative assessment of meaning between a written statement and a visual one can be another valuable exercise for an English teacher, for example, in a written essay upon *Work* compared to a sequence of photographs that have dealt also with this topic. The important point here is that we can hope to use a double system of communication, the useful abstraction that, in essence, a word is, and the more concrete example of a photograph. Though the photograph, like the word, is merely a description of an event, for most people it represents the event itself. By its use the teacher can direct the attention of his class to the particular and check any pupil's tendency to theorize loosely. In fact, requiring each pupil in a group to describe a photograph (used in this context as a substitute for a real event) would reveal immediately the different values each child ascribes to the same terms, and open up a good discussion. Eric Bentley writes, 'Our perception is riveted to need. Our real needs being relatively few, our perceptions are few.' Thus, the teacher of English may recognise that he cannot be simply responsible for helping those prompted by apparent need to read and write but also must assist others in identifying their own goals and desires. It is surely a mistake to think of language as an end in itself, and not as a tool.

WORD AND IMAGE

The meaning of any word can be given by other words, or by demonstration. Thus, I might tell you a spade is a digging tool, or show you a spade. A form of dumbshow or mime, of course, may prove enough to convey my meaning. It would be impracticable to fill the classroom with actual objects for any length of time, but an empiric approach to learning the meaning of words can be adopted, and filmstock can be used purposefully in the process. Consider these words: *Slither Skid Slide Slip*. Is there a demonstrable difference between each? If the teacher believes that it is important that members of his class discover that interpretations of words may vary according to the individual he can prove it by this experiment. A camera can be used here to record the efforts of his pupils.

CONCEPT AND IMAGE

A concept or general notion can be examined in a similar manner. 'What is war?' Practical demonstration in this instance can hardly exceed stylised representations in dramatic performance. But there is a useful source of pictures of real events to be taken from the colour supplements of certain newspapers, or lavishly illustrated magazines such as *Life* and *Paris Match*. From these a pupil can be called upon to identify by word, or concept, what he sees in the picture.

Extension of concept and image exercise

The use of cut-outs has already been commented upon in the text. After a sequence of cut-out images has been chosen they can be filmed by the *rostrum* camera method. The group's project on *Laughter,* described on page 68 used carefully selected images of people laughing as a 'talking point' during their enquiry into the nature of human laughter. Indeed there are excellent opportunities to use such material in helping young children to form concepts of what makes up their environment.

IDENTIFICATION EXERCISES

The magazine materials that can be used in the classroom are natural teaching aids, found in many homes throughout the country. Too often, the visual display material produced by an educational authority bears for many children the stigma of being purely instructional, it smacks of

134

the schoolroom and may cause a child to lose interest. To use material with which children are familiar makes it possible to deal with what features predominantly in their lives but is not necessarily understood by them. Consequently, pictures from magazines can be taken, the subjects identified, and the teacher can direct the exercise as he chooses.

In explaining the parts of speech of the English language, virtually any cut-out picture can be used: What nouns can we use to describe those seen in the picture? Man, Woman, Bed, etc. And verbs? Bending, smoking. Bending OVER—what kind of word is 'over'? And adjectives? The picture can be systematically analyzed, and the words finally used in a written description of the scene. The teacher might also ask his pupils to write an exciting narrative around the picture itself: What happened to this man? Almost every picture has an element of mystery: Where is it? Who is it? A teacher can exploit this with profit. Two pictures carefully joined can create a place 'out of this world'. Figures can be easily transported to other regions. Even a conventional view, cut-out or postcard, can provide the basis for a useful written exercise.

The pupil may be asked to accept that he has just arrived in the spot shown in the picture you have given him. Is he on holiday? Does he own these premises? Ask him to write a description of how he arrived. The results will not necessarily be mundane. For example:

Holidaze
Here I am in a helicopter ready for my two week stay in Arabia. The sun is beating on my back through the glass roof. The helicopter goes down to ground.
I didn't know what was going on. He stopped his engine and took my suitcase out:
'I hope you have a nice stay'.
The helicopter started and took off. He left me standing in the middle of an Arabian desert: no human in sight; no buildings; no nothing. The sun was beating on me. When he said a mystery tour I thought it would be fun, but this is going too far.
I opened my case and found a shrivelled up fish.

Tony Weston

135–137

DIALOGUE EXERCISES USING IMAGES AS A SPRINGBOARD TO DRAMATIC DIALOGUE

In the exercise illustrated below, pupils were asked to invent a possible dialogue between the man and the boy. The old lady soliloquizes upon her predicament; the members of the class might be set the task of tracing other characters out of magazines who are part of her story, ie the heartless son, the money-grubbing landlord etc. The class can be set to work with the assurance that all, heroes and villains alike, are present somewhere in pictorial form in these magazines.

Such exercises as these might be regarded as a means of developing a pupil's ability to have empathetic relationships with others, although these feelings cannot be forced. The most important aspect of these activities is that a dialogue takes place. For example, it is not necessary to depend upon human figures; but features, merely or anthropomorphic devices can be employed as a means of evoking words.

138–140

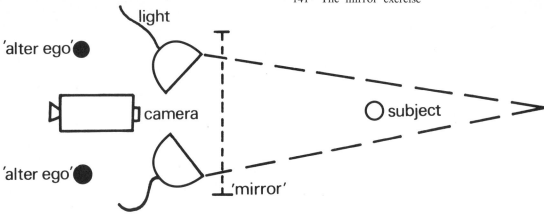

'light'

'alter ego' ●

'alter ego' ●

camera

subject

'mirror'

In the classroom it is possible to create a film-stage (see sketches A and B) by carefully angling the light to illuminate the desired area and subject, and hide the unwanted view of furniture and audience. A stage spotlight is the most effective means of accomplishing this kind of set, but ordinary lighting can be modified by using an improvised reflector.

A dialogue between a number of pupils can easily be launched by using such a simple prop as a telephone with a tape-recorder running under the table. This exercise aims to produce sequences of words according to the topic chosen by class or teacher, but a camera can record the facial expressions of the speakers, and later the transcribed statements can be matched to the appropriate expression. This form of exercise is well suited to the classroom film-stage, the action, of necessity, must be carefully controlled and not allowed to move through the surrounding wall of darkness.

In sketch B, a cardboard oval framed to represent a mirror, is placed before a subject, and he or she is invited to speak to the countenance seen, to soliloquize or reflect upon personal fortunes. Behind the mirror sit other pupils acting as answering voices or alter egos; they are concealed from the principal subject by a light shining through the frame, making it impossible to see through the mirror. While a tape-recorder can be used to record the dialogue, the face of the well-lit subject can easily be photographed. An exercise of this kind can assist the teacher when he feels that the members of his group may benefit by discussions of personal aspirations and behaviour. A talking-out in this manner can read as follows:

AE It's part of growing up.
C   They always say that. Part of growing up, it's not though. It's something that happens to *you*. Might be a part of growing up to them, but it's something special to you.
AE They *have felt* the same.
C   No two people can feel the same about something like that.
AE You're just full of self-pity!
C   Yes, and they all say that too. Perhaps it's true.
AE Yes, they're always talking about you. They don't understand you.
C   There's not much to understand.
AE They don't realize that.
C   Just a person like everybody else. They don't like me.
AE They think you're different. They don't understand you *at all!*
C   Of course, when I look into the mirror I see something different again. Depending upon what sort of mood I'm in. When I'm happy there's a change altogether. It changes your whole face when you're happy. Not when you're like this. Makes me want to look away.
AE Go on! Smile!
C   Smile! That changes the face but not the eyes. Don't like my eyes. Not tonight.

Caroline Neuburg, Lydia Heller, Linden Salter

So far dealt with is the use of a picture image as a starting point to story, poem or dialogue exercises. There is another important, frequently neglected, usage to consider, the written or printed word itself as a visual image. The word *sun* printed in fifty styles, gives fifty different images of that word. Art teachers find this significant, but it seems unlikely that many English teachers would use this exercise in their teaching. Yet, between the art teacher's interest in graphics as a form of pattern-making and drawing exercise, and the English teacher's assumption of the responsibility for seeing that the child writes neatly and clearly, there is a vast no-man's-land where no-one has ventured to examine possibilities of what might be achieved by writing language more *expressively*. Clearly, the emotive force of language can depend upon the style of writing and the materials on which the inscriptions are made.

It is possible to think of the blank page as a stage upon which words will perform. Fanciful as this may seem there is a satisfaction in writing if statements have been expressed clearly and forcefully and are not marred by deletions. It seems a sad fact that many pupil's exercise books bear evidence of what the teacher has felt, that only a certain style of writing would do. The book may give only a record of struggle between teacher and pupil, and contain little that the owner would regard as a personal accomplishment to be kept, to be shown and enjoyed by others. For many teachers, an exercise book to be proud of is judged by the standard of marking and neatness. But what else might the pupil wish to see in his book that might enhance its value to him? Typescript rather than handwriting? Illustrations and photographs? Might it not become something of a scrapbook as well? It is too easy for the exercise book to become a kind of conduct sheet with marks for and against the pupil; were it to have a more positive function, the pupil might be given a greater responsibility for filling it with work that can interest readers other than himself or the teacher.

142–144

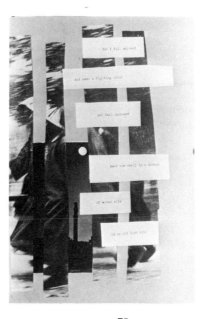

Why confine writing to the page? Dare we consider changing the contours of the traditional format? Certainly if we are interested in expanding the visual content of English teaching we will want to experiment. Most people too readily accept the traditional boundaries that confine our writing to the page, the book, and the library shelf. Are present standards of literature likely to be jeopardized if pupils are encouraged to create their own rules and write creatively? The term *creative writing* is often used to describe the effort made by individuals to write what and how they please, to produce entirely personal statements. It is just as important to recognise the creative writing exercise as a useful antidote for the tight-lacing of the mind which happens too frequently to the pupil taking an academic course; it may also stimulate the pupil bored by, or fearful of, the act of writing.

With this freedom the writer might look to not only writing *for* the screen, but *on* the screen. Today, is an age when the word can be 'writ large' as never before, and young people are likely to appreciate the chance to exploit such an opportunity.

Changing the contours of the classical format
Writing upon walls, needless to say, is a different delight from writing upon paper. Bertolt Brecht described his use of film screens on which texts were flashed as a play was being performed as the *transliteration of the stage.* It is possible to enlist pupils' help in 'transliterating' the classroom by pinning sheets of paper on walls, desks, floor and ceiling and making a plentiful supply of felt tip pens available to them. With a given subject each pupil may write on a separate sheet, or, the exercise can be organized as a group activity with all pupils writing where they wish, the process becoming, in effect, one of statement and counter-statement. The results may be exploited variously. For example, the transliterated section of the room can be treated as a stage 'dressed' for performance, with the texts on display both to audience, as declarations upon the subject of the performance; and to actor as 'cues' upon which to improvise.

Change the shape of a page, and present a challenge to your pupils. Give each a writing book, access to a typewriter and *carte blanche* with illustration and layout, and a greater concern for what goes between its covers might result. With single sheets of paper an alteration of shape can be made to achieve a visual effect. For example, if children are asked to write about the sun, each page can be cut into the shape of the sun. When the individual efforts are collected they can be placed together on a table and by forming different constellations varying word sequences emerge. Such exercises as these were the delight of the Dada-ists of the Cabaret Voltaire in Zurich in the nineteen-twenties. They were also interested in *collage* which, again, offers the opportunity for exercises in relating word and image.

COLLAGE AND MONTAGE

Most teachers with an interest in film-making are likely to have discussed Sergei Eisenstein's theory of *Montage,* that is, the effect achieved when two pieces of film joined together, inevitably combine into a new concept, a new quality arising out of that juxtaposition. This means that if shown one film image, and then shown another, 'a new quality' relating to both of these will be discovered in the image that succeeds them. Nevertheless, Eisenstein regarded montage as a method of pictorial representation which allowed him to calculate the effect upon the viewer. His theory is a sophisticated tool for use by the film-maker, particularly the propagandist. It is important to remember this when examining the related method of picture juxtaposing commonly known as *collage.*

Collage is usually treated as a display medium, but the collage film is a possibility. Both *collage* and *montage* share the aim of creating new qualities through the juxtaposing of the known. The dividing principle is to be found in the selection of images: *Montage* means a careful selection; *Collage* makes 'discoveries' through a random placing together of images. It is this randomness that is the essence of the activity. A *collage* may be understood to represent the order or non-order that exists in the maker's life. By achieving a visual display of this flux of people, places, things, and ideas it becomes possible to contemplate and search for what might exist but be hidden from the human consciousness in everyday life. In effect, the artist sets out to explore the relativity of human events.

80

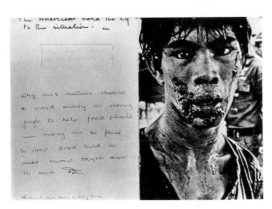

145–147 My Vietnam autograph book

The word collage

We have already considered what brings us to by-pass the rules and experiment freely with words. Shakespeare's sonnet 'Shall I compare thee to a summer's day?' is probably as indestructible, short of a nuclear holocaust, as any great poem. The student who dismantled it felt no sense of doing more than attempting to use words outside his usual vocabulary:

> Thou wander'st long and lovely when fair buds owest,
> Hot chance, that every fair darling gives
> And sometimes declines short breathe and of course
> The eye in heaven can see thee.

The result is a parody, at best; but, more important for the student, it is an active experience of the words rather than a forced act of idolatry. He has attempted more than a reading of the poem.

In the above exercise the student began by writing each word of the poem on slips of paper, scattering these, and re-assembling them at random. The act of random association of words can be developed around chosen pictures, with each picture-word mass finally merging together into a total whirl of words. From these lines can be extracted or traced lineally in various directions until the writer achieves a result which satisfies himself, and a concatenation of words and images that may surprise and delight the viewer.

If the teacher wishes to bring an important issue to the attention of his class, another possible use of *collage* is to gather evidence of the flux of opinions held within the school group by collecting written statements in a book designed as a visual stimulus. In the example shown, pictures of the Vietnam war were pasted into a discarded brochure, and colleagues and students approached with the request to 'write something in my Vietnam autograph book'. The result was a myriad body of opinions, itself reflecting the complexity of the situation. The teacher must find supplies of brochures for this kind of conversion exercise where he can; banks and tourist agencies are excellent sources of free material.

A collage project

In the exercise described above a comparison of views was made by collecting written statements and discussing these in the classroom. It was anticipated by the collector from the outset that sharply differing views would be expressed. This same subject, the war in Vietnam, was studied more fully by a young girl, Ann Scott, who also recognized that a wide variance of viewpoints exist. Her aim was to juxtapose all shades of opinion; to attempt a collage presentation of these, and by doing this she was obliged to gather a great deal of printed matter, recorded statements, photographs and picture material from magazines.

Her first step was to construct a portable *frieze* of pictures of the events of the war, designed to be hung on the wall of her room, or any other room she visited. While invited guests looked at these, she conducted a running interview, asking each interviewee for a declaration of personal feeling *à propos* a particular picture. Later, she filmed this *frieze*, and most of her 8mm film material was inserted into cassettes for use with a *loop* projector.

Next, a sound collage composed of headlines from English and American newspapers was tape-recorded, and this, essentially, was a statement of her own feelings:

WARSAW powers pledge on volunteers for
  VIETNAM
Plea for US restraint on HANOI threat
BRITISH apathy
The Communist menace
HANOI grow weary of war says Ball
ATTACKS WILL CONTINUE

Her third step was a detailed analysis of the press reports, which were separated under these headings:

1 The area of war
   a What soldiers do to each other in battle
   b What soldiers do to civilians
2 Statements made by those in the war that are intended to describe why it is happening:
   a The military personnel
   b The politicians
   c The Vietnamese civilians North and South
   d The American civilians

These statements were extracted from various papers and journals, mounted on sheets of cards and displayed. Something of the wide divergence of opinion on the war could be obtained by studying this *collage*.

Finally, she took many of the questions that emerged from this form of enquiry to various information agencies, left-wing political groups and the US Embassy publicity officer. Again, in order to attempt to understand her own motives, or, perhaps it might be said, her own understanding of the war, she preceded this last visit by talking into a tape-recorder herself, being presented with subject headings by others and asked to talk spontaneously and immediately into the microphone.

Given the importance of this issue, Ann needed to make excursions which she would not have had time for within an average hour-long period of the English lesson. Obviously, in the classroom she could have spent the hour discussing the issues involved in writing an essay upon the subject. But surely it is necessary to question the time-tabling, and the actual provision made to enable pupils to carry out work rather than declare such a project as impracticable or time-wasting.

The walls of any classroom are potentially projection screens or display panels. They are also, if bare and light-coloured, a very large page upon which the pupils can write, draw, or paste cut-out materials. (And if the room is cleared of desks, the floor too can become a page.) If the headmaster, principal, or school inspector is likely to cry desecration, make sure they do know about modern, washable wall paints and fillers, water-soluble inks and mounting pastes. In fact, it takes very little time to wash a *collage* from a wall if such a paste has been used.

The following project was carried out on a wall approximately 18 feet high and 40 feet in length. It was bare except for a door at each end with a clock on one of them. The decision was made to create a *collage,* with each student taking responsibility for a major section, and each student undertaking the making of a film which would embody both images photographed directly from the collage, and subjects filmed in the street. The final product we hoped was to be, in effect, a collage film.

With the overall theme accepted as 'the human situation' fourteen ancillary themes were each designated to a particular position on the wall:

Death, Old age, The night city, Pleasure, Poverty, Personal tragedy, The dream, Human groups, Religion, Politics, War, Love, Motherhood, The origins of humans.

Each student undertook to complete and link his or her panel with the surrounding areas. The mechanics of the exercise were simple:

1 Selection of material from magazines, etc.
2 Mixing of *Polycell* (a wallpaper paste) 'bath', old film cans filled with this solution being found the easiest means of each student having his individual 'palette'. The cut-out picture was totally immersed in the solution and smoothed on to the wall, 'massaging' being necessary to remove all air bubbles from underneath.

The actual preparation of the *collage* took longer than anticipated and proved to be an exhausting task. When it was finished, filming took place.

When a person first looks at a *collage* it is likely that his eye will be taken by a particular image, and from there his vision will travel, following a dominant line of images or, perhaps, a sense of movement created by the angling of the pictures. Again, simply a flow of images of like colour and shading can be enough to steer the attention of the viewer. However, as these rhythms and lines cross and interweave the human eye is compelled to switch and search in various directions. Thus, the aim is achieved of bringing the onlooker to ponder the associations that exist between phenomena.

Each member of the group was asked to film the dominant rhythms of his own section of the *collage,* and relate these to the film passages shot afterwards in the street. For example, the film of the *religion* section was finally intercut with shots taken both outside and inside London churches. In the outdoors filming, short shots of 9 to 10 frames each were taken, and the camera frequently tilted to photograph the subjects from different angles. Thus, on projection of the film onto a screen at normal speed, 18 frames per second, the images gyrated rapidly and a collage effect was achieved. The superimposition of image upon image in the camera is another valuable effect which can be employed by those interested in collage film-making.

Film editors are responsible for cutting film into sequences and arranging these in an order which best tells the story, if it is a screenplay, or demonstrates the event that actually happened, if it is a documentary film. Throughout their work, they have to make fine judgments with their eyes, ears, and head. In all forms of film editing, continuity of sense and action are important. Can the young would-be film-maker find trimming and matching cut-out pictures from magazines a form of practice that will later help him to edit films? It seems certain that a pupil in matching and cutting images carefully or grading the colour tones between pictures will exercise those faculties he will employ in actual film editing. Creating a narrative or documentary sequence out of a limited number of pictures (but not too limited!) which has a verbal and visual logic is a problem which faces any professional film-maker.

In order to create a picture story out of a number of magazine pictures that have no relationship to each other, the cutter needs a strong sense of narrative, a keen eye and a steady hand. His principal task is to establish a relationship between each picture. To do this he will certainly have to be prepared to alter drastically the size of a picture, and to find a point at which he can cut in order to reduce it to resemble the preceding image. If, for example, a sequence involving a moving white car is envisaged, all the pictures of white cars that can be found must be assembled, then each picture must be trimmed until the sequence conveys the impression of a white car making a journey. In this armchair form of film-making (such sequences, of course, can later be filmed) the convention of a variable screen or picture size has to be accepted.

It is also possible by using cut-outs to demonstrate many of the basic terms used in film-making, though, perhaps the most effective exercise is to give your pupils scissors and magazines and ask them to cut pictures to shapes and sizes that will delineate the meaning of such terms as *the close-up, panning,* etc. The sense of this exercise is based on the simple fact that the human eye can move in closer to detail, retreat or scan horizontally and vertically over the scene, in other words behave quite naturally as the camera eye might if moved by your hands.

The story sequence

The paste-up of a story from cut-outs can be performed with several ends in view. It might be regarded as a method of scripting, ie a form of story-board making; or, the mounting of a picture sequence might be done in order to produce a picture story. After mounting, the book can be pinned open page by page upon a board and filmed by the rostrum camera method. This will only be practicable if the pictures are of adequate size to be filmed, and should be at least 254mm (10 in.) by 200mm (8 in.).

In the first example shown, *The Gamblers,* the making of a picture story book was intended. In this exercise the cutter was concerned solely with matching the pictures according to subject or colour. Thus, a procedure of reducing each picture, of eliminating unrequired features, was carried out by cutting carefully until the requisite action had been framed. In this exercise it is hoped that the eye of the viewer will make the necessary adjustment to the variable size of screen, rather than demand the consistent dimension of frame found in the cinema.

The second example shows yet another story-board sequence in which a standard size of picture has been maintained throughout, thus enabling the cutter to film these pictures at a later date. After filming had been completed by the rostrum camera method, a sound track was prepared. The girl who was asked to record the written commentary, that is, to read the captions printed under the pictures in the book, was placed before a screen with a tape-recorder and record-player beside her. These were controlled by an operator. Next, the projector was moved to a position just outside the door of the room to eliminate the risk of the microphone recording its noise while running. The projector and tape-recorder were started simultaneously from a point where both film and tape had been marked with a chinagraph pencil. (This kind of pencil will write upon polished surfaces.) As each image appeared on the screen the girl read the matching caption into the microphone to the accompanying background of the music of Elgar and Arnold. The recording level and volume of music were controlled by the operator, responsible, in effect, for mixing the voice and music before the microphone. On restarting both projector and recorder from the marks, a synchronization of image and sound was achieved.

In the third exercise, illustrated below, an actual cutting together of two or more pictures was attempted. Again, the aim was to match pictures by size and colour. This sequence was prepared for children and tells the story of an unhappy man summoned to the kingdom of birds. After these *collage* pictures had been made, they were photographed with a 35mm camera, using Kodachrome II slide film. For this kind of work it is important that a camera with a reflex viewer be used, in order that the user can photograph exactly what he sees in the viewfinder. A slide projector, such as the Kodak *Carousel* enables the story-teller to screen slide after slide controlling the machine by remote switch control whilst talking to his group. Again, a sound-track can be prepared and the projector operated according to pre-determined cues from the tape-recorder.

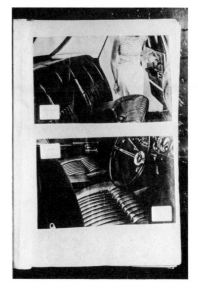

154   Gambling bores me
       I am ready

155   At his signal
       To leave

156   A diplomat
       Is given
       Big
       Fast
       Cars

157   We drive
       Fast
       I learned

158   To care for him
       Very much

159   Early in our relationship
       Being together

160   At the Bird King's summons

161   He leaves at once

162   Soaring over the city

163   Over rivers and lakes

164   Through the doors of the Bird Heaven

165   Up to the Bird King's royal chamber

A WRITING EXERCISE USING THE 8 mm CAMERA AS AN AID

Each beginning of an academic year brings with it the prospect of new classes little known or unknown to the teacher. The question of how willingly and successfully these classes are likely to work is one of considerable concern to most teachers.

For the new teacher, in particular, the problem can be formidable. His likely uncertainty as to how to present his facts, how to teach, will be matched probably by an equal degree of uncertainty about personal approach, how he is to deal as a person with his own class. The frequent counsel, 'to get a grip on them before they get a grip on you' may well conflict with his own ideas about teaching. He is unlikely to lack for advice, albeit kindly intended; but for many young teachers a measure of their own potential in their own terms is what they are striving for. This is more likely to be gained, as most will realize, through actual teaching experience rather than demonstration and advice by other teachers, valuable though this must be. Unless the young teacher is involved in team teaching from the start of his career, he will enter a classroom on his first day faced with a possible thirty to forty complex of new relationships.

For many who find themselves in this position, the most seemingly sensible step is to rely upon the largely theoretical how-to-do-it instruction of teacher training and advice from more experienced colleagues. An alternative to this course is to make a completely empiric approach: to try from the beginning of your association with your pupils to learn something of their ambitions and fears and base lessons upon such findings.

How can the 8mm camera be put to work during a course of English, when your actual wish is to gauge your pupils' sympathies before offering them instruction in film-making? The following account describes a second and third lesson at the start of a school year in which the 8mm camera was employed to achieve this goal.

Time September 1967
Place A college of further education, London
Group Twenty-one 16 to 18-year-old girls taking a professional secretarial training course
Subject English. One hour periods

Aim To involve all in describing the experience of arriving at the college for the first time

At our first meeting there had been time only for an introductory chat. This was to be our second lesson. My immediate proposal was that we discuss the problems each of us had met with in being new to the college. What had it really been like to walk through the college gates bound for lessons for the first time? Only three days had elapsed since each one of us had done so. Surely, it was still very fresh in everyone's mind?

I produced the 8mm camera—and two *Kodak* box cameras and suggested that we leave the college and attempt to re-enact those arrivals of that first morning. One of the girls agreed to film our re-creation of the event. Later we agreed we could study our film and discuss how successful it was as a piece of historical interpretation.

They were interested; the camera gave them an *out*, a break from the classroom. Because their training was largely desk-based and dull, they were glad to be involved in such an activity, to take part in an event.

The camera possessed a built-in exposure meter and simple focusing devices. No-one confessed to any experience of film-making, but less than three minutes were taken to explain the camera's workings to the volunteer cameraman. Our schedule had to conform to the hour-long teaching period, a circumstance which generally lends itself to a high risk of out-of-focus shooting. Nevertheless, pre-performance elaboration upon techniques and possible mistakes must be avoided at first in order to bring the technically and non-technically minded elements of the group together to produce photographs and films. With simple-to-use equipment, results in terms of films can be quickly produced.

We left our third floor classroom and made for the main hall. A number of students and members of staff were in sight, and we were conscious to some degree of the curious, and sometimes baffled, stares of passers-by. I divided the class into two groups, A and B. Unit A started and filmed a progress from a short distance outside the college gates to an assembly point within the main entrance hall. On both sides of the main door unit B photographed entries and calls upon the college enquiry office. After both groups had shot the amount of film allotted to each they

RIES ↗

166

exchanged cameras and switched locations: B filmed an approach to the college and A concentrated upon interior work.

Each group had been given 7.6 metres (25 feet) of 8mm film and one roll of tri-X 120 film. The college is a modern building with much glass panelling and filming inside the entrance hall was possible. Each unit made a sequential progress, filming carefully, and my role was limited to being on hand for consultation if required. I was not needed. Simple equipment was being used and the pace and rhythm of the exercise allowed all to be involved continuously.

The entire enterprise took the hour available to us, and no time was left for a discussion of our efforts.

At our next meeting, two days later, I returned to the subject of our first-day experience. I asked each girl to record what had happened to herself moment by moment; to remember as if the brain was a slow motion camera. On the previous Monday we had recorded our movements and expressions of emotion in detail with a camera; now I asked them to write as carefully as a camera records. The camera observes the particular; a photograph is specific. How specific can one be in using language?

> The wind blew and I felt my hair sliding across my face. I brushed it back behind my ears. I looked at the building a few yards ahead of me. All the time I talked with my three friends. This was a way of concealing my nervousness. I saw steps ahead and prepared myself to climb them. There was one big step in the middle. I thought of it as an intermission. It was a break between the two difficult bits. I noticed the linkway between the two big buildings. It reminded me of the one at school and I expected to see the familiar benches and coat hangers. There were none. This wasn't my old school. Immediately a problem confronted me. There were several doors. Which one was I to choose? Hell! I don't want to look a fool by opening the wrong one. An answer came. I bent down and played with my shoe strap, enabling my friend with the red dress and long black hair to take the lead. She chose the wrong door, making a joke out of it. As I turned to look and laugh with my other two friends I noticed a crowd of 'with it' girls behind. They would soon be with us; overtaking us. The laughing had to stop. It did.
> *Bernadette Guinane*

The door opened quickly and silently, I

90

expected it to creak, not with age, but newness. I walked straight to the back of the class not knowing consciously why I did so; the logical explanation would be that the other desks had been already filled, but as I remember the back desk caught my eye first and I went to it directly not even seeing the other desks or students.

I sat down, smoothed out my skirt and brushed back a stray hair from my face. It was at this point that I began to be aware of my fellow students, the other furniture and the tutor. I liked her immediately, feeling secretly glad that she also took us for shorthand. My eyes wandered to the outside. Being on the top floor I could see the tree tops; it was windy; there were no birds.

Susan Roe

I took my tray and pushed it along. First I collected my pudding, then came my first course. Not noticing the menu by the door I had the first thing I saw. I could feel people's eyes watching me. I moved slowly on, paid for my dinner and went to sit down. Everything had seemed to go off quite well until I realised I had forgotten my knife and fork.

Susan Le Feuvre

Almost all of the accounts were clearly and precisely written. In one piece the action had been absurdly slowed down. 'I walked on towards the thirteenth step. When I reached it I lifted my foot off the ground.' Two were flippant in tone, the writers giving more consideration to joke-telling than reporting. But essentially the language used was simple and functional. It was possible to see in the detailing of action succeeding action, emotion succeeding emotion, the basic form of a film script.

One factor of considerable significance emerged from our experiment. Almost every account spoke of a shyness, a fear of new places. In subsequent readings the pieces were listened to in such a way as to indicate that each girl was enormously reassured to learn that she had not been alone in her feelings and attitudes of that first day. The camera exercise had introduced more than an exciting approach to our English lessons. The members of the class through this experience had discovered the feelings of confidence and doubt they shared, in common, and so had the teacher.

167

THE PORTABLE TAPE-RECORDER

The tape-recorder and the camera can be regarded as tools with a common purpose: the recording of physical events, both actions and words. After use, the camera retains images of seen action; conversely, the tape-recorder holds heard words and sounds. This similarity of function means that many of the exercises similar to those undertaken with the camera described in this text can be performed with the portable tape-recorder.

These machines can be carried easily by the pupil (especially those of the *Phillips* cassette variety which fit into an overcoat pocket) and might therefore become an accessory he carries for use at any time during the day. By this arrangement the pupil bears with him or her the means of instantly recording conversation, or his own thoughts and feelings, which itself may be regarded as a form of writing.

One pupil, Keith O'Hagen, at an early age became interested in the tape-recorder and would spend long periods talking into the microphone. Today, it is a machine into which he can talk naturally with a determination not to stop before his intended statement has been made. For him, this method of verbalizing his thoughts, of instantaneous writing in fact, has stimulated an enthusiasm to use words that might not have happened had he been dependent upon waiting for his written work to be marked and returned by his teachers.

The direct writing of a story:

The Railway tunnel
I was lost.
I was completely lost.
I didn't know where I was, what time it was, or what day it was.
I was all alone. Wandering, down the Piccadilly line, sometime at night. I think it was the Piccadilly line, it looked like it, but then, all underground stations look the same to me. But I remember walking down there, all on my own, and suddenly, a train started coming towards me I didn't know what to do!
So, I just laid down a bit, and I thought 'it's bound to go away in a minute'.
But it didn't. It went straight over me.
When it'd gone I got up, and suddenly,
I wasn't down in the underground station any more.
And I wasn't lost any more.
I was at home, sitting in a chair.
And it was half past three. And it was a Sunday! And it was March 15th! And my Mum was sitting there doing her knitting, it was my Mum! And my Dad was outside cleaning the car. And my brother was playing with his toy cars! And my sister, was upstairs in bed with her boyfriend. And I picked up the paper. And I read it. On the front page was something strange. Something, that might have even happened to me. It was a headline, a boy, and, you've probably guessed. He was lost. Down an underground railway station, just like what happened to me! And he didn't know what time it was! And he didn't know where he was! And he thought it was the Piccadilly line, but they all look the bloody same!
They all look the bloody same! Underground lines all look the same.
And then, something strange happened to him. A train started coming towards him. And he laid down. And the train went over him and killed him.
And I larfed. Because I'd got away. I'd got

away and, I put the paper down, and I went out and made a cup of tea in the kitchen. And my Mum said: 'Make one for me'. And my Dad come in, and he said: 'Mind the train'!

A talent for mimicry enables him to introduce characters in his dialogues. And to re-create conversations held earlier:

Light an' bitter, please (*drinks*)
Silence
(*drawling, 'stagey' voice of woman*) He-ello. What's your name?
Oh, my name's er, Keith.
O-ohh, (*pause*) My name's Joyce.
Oh, pleased to meet yer.
Ah haven't seen you in here before?
No, I'm only up here for the day, you know, jus sort of walkin' around like, y-you know?
Ohh. I'm always here.
Are you? Very nice, too.
Are you alone or with a friend?
Oh no, I'm on me own, no, jus thought I'd go awt, somewhere to go, you know, something to do.
Oh, that's nice. Is that a camera you've got there?
Yeah, oh year.
What sort of pictures do you take?
Oh, anything really, you know anything, you know, what I mean?
Oh, how lovely! Do you ever take photos of, um, people?
Oh, yes, sometimes, yes, well you can take them of anything, y'know people, flowers, trees . . .
Oooh. I say would you like to take some photos of me?
Well (*giggles*) dunno really.
Oh, but would you? You could come back to my flat if you like.
What? Now?
Well, when you've finished your drink of course. Y'know, if you'd like to buy me another one.
Oh, all right then, do you live very far from here?
Ooh no, not very far really, just down the road, only just round the corner.
Oh alright, I'll have a . . .
Oooh, I'll have a gin I think . . .
Right, gin and another pint, please . . .

This conversation was re-created several hours

after meeting Joyce, a most colourful cigar-smoking lady seated at a bar in the West End of London. Keith was able to translate the experience into a recording in which he captured most of the comicality and pathos of the real event. Perhaps, the most significant aspect of this exercise was that Keith not only proved himself to be sensitive to another's use of language, but revealed his awareness of his own speech patterns.

If the teacher of English recognises a value to the pupil in being involved in making discoveries about *his own use* of words, then the portable tape-recorder will prove to be an invaluable tool. After listening to a recording made by himself a pupil can be asked to comment upon any number of aspects of his use of language, Any misrepresentations, inversions and elliptical phrasing can be identified if desired by this method. But, more important, he can be asked, 'How clearly have you said what you wished to say?' This effectively is to pose the question, 'Can you use language to describe what you want?' For many pupils it is difficult to use words to describe what they want because they want a great deal. The problem is exemplified by the words of Keith's friend who said, 'What I think I can't say, and what I say I usually don't mean.'

A FILM PORTRAIT

A short documentary film portrait of a young girl was attempted, using the portable tape-recorder to create the sound-track as the actual shooting took place. It was agreed that she was to walk through the streets of central London closely followed by the cameraman whom she would ignore until he spoke to her. A portable tape-recorder was placed in her shoulder bag and the microphone clipped to its strap at shoulder level. The cameraman had the dual responsibility of photographing her progress, and periodically catching up with her to give her subject headings (see below) upon which she immediately recorded statements as she continued walking. During her soliloquies the cameraman refrained from filming until she had completed her recording. The girl was called upon to give all her attention to her journey through the streets and was always under some strain in waiting for her next cue. It was hoped that these statements might be truer to her

feelings or at least less modified than statements made before a microphone in a studio. It is only possible to give extracts from this sound track:

Teachers
I seem to forget that teachers are people too, can't imagine some of them actually living a family life, actually being human beings. They're just there to spout facts, some of them don't even care whether you understand or not. They just do their job, talk and talk, and they're satisfied.

Old People
Sometimes I feel as though I agree with those heartless souls who say that the very old should be shot, got rid of, they're no good. This is mainly because when I see them walking around the streets it really upsets me. So old they can't cross the road, can't see properly, can't hear properly, can't eat, nothing. But then I think of the old people I know. I realise the thought of them being shot is just ridiculous.

Beatles
I used to like them when I was younger. I used to scream at them. Don't any more. Don't scream at anything.

This exercise was used to enable the girl to make truthful statements of her feelings on a number of topics. The actual journey distracted her sufficiently from making those corrections to her statements which might have finally produced better prose but would have seriously interfered with the balance of feeling that was expressed.

Finally, she arrived in Trafalgar Square and talked of an experience she remembered from a previous occasion:

... the minute we sat down two policemen came dashing over to make sure we weren't pushing drugs, and then one of them claimed he'd seen me before, and when had I last been there? We discovered eventually that it was when I took my French pen-friend to Downing Street and starting talking to this policeman, and he asked me to the policemen's ball, it was him! He looked me up in his little notebook to see if I had been on any drugs charges or anything thrilling like that. It was only when he said 'I've seen you somewhere before' I said, 'I only know one policeman and that's the one who stands outside Downing Street' and

168   Quality goods

169   Servants
170   Chauffeurs

suddenly he realised. I suppose it's beneath their dignity to apologise, makes them appear like human beings with weaknesses, who can make mistakes.

It is possible to use this method of recording to direct the subject's attention to aspects of the locality through which he or she is passing. Mayfair, one of London's most expensive areas, was chosen as a location for a girl to walk through, in the manner described above, again, followed by the cameraman:

Quality goods
This is the area to find them: everything sold here has to have 'quality'. There is too much luxury here. It's marvellous to look in shop windows and see all the expensive goods you don't need, and know you don't need them. Buying quality is probably a vital need for the people who live or work in Mayfair.

Servants
Do people still have servants? I wouldn't like to be a servant to anyone. I always think of rich, spoilt people having to be helped into their clothes, dressed!, or being curtsied to, it's positively unhealthy. Everybody *needs* to be able to take care of themselves. Only the sick or inadequate should need servants really.

Chauffeurs
Servants are status symbols. Do their employers confide in them as some women do with their hairdresser? I suppose having the Rolls for the day means you can play the lord and pretend you are rich yourself. Some people would enjoy that. It could be an opportunity to lead a double life.

If a transcription of this type of recording takes place, a desk-based activity, the moment arrives for the pupil to look closely at his work. It seems pointless to consider its marking in the traditional manner, but a discussion that is directly concerned with how language has been used by this or that person can prove instructive. The elliptical phrasing of the girl's statements about *teachers* and *old people* reveals how thoughts can be expressed in simple, direct, statements. Relating language directly to experience, saying neither more nor less than what has to be said is instructive to both teacher and pupils.

Under the terms of the *Camera Adventure* exercise a teacher may send his pupils out into the street to raise topics with the people they meet which are both unquestionably difficult to introduce and to discuss. A group of young people, sent into the dock area of East London to ask people, 'What does the word *love* mean to you?' were obliged to find answers quickly when their interviewees asked, inevitably, 'Why do you want to know?' It only becomes possible to ask such questions if you are bold, in earnest, and readily grateful for any attention received. These young people were; and the seamen, dockers and other residents of the area responded generously and with good humour. Nevertheless, anyone who ventured to ask this question usually had to provide a number of answers before being able to ask any further questions. It was necessary for these sixteen-year-olds to use their own words to explain their unusual request, and what results were anticipated from the exercise. In fact, the group had not been prepared in advance for the subject with which they dealt, nor told of the area they were to visit. Thus, each could only depend upon his or her powers of speech to see them through the afternoon.

They were asked to record whatever evidence of love they could find. A printed sheet containing several writers' definitions of love was given to each member, accompanied by a guide sheet outlining the specific working zones, and offering the following categories as an indication of what might be looked for:

a Manifestations (of love): that which may be easily seen by the eye or perceived by the mind.

'the eye' must look, see, record with the camera.

'the mind' must think, ask, and tape-record.

Manifestations are obvious examples, eg loving couples, mothers and babies, etc.

b Tokens (of love): a sign, an indication, material manifestations in fact, eg Mother's day cards, writing on walls etc.

The final result was a collection of photographs, rolls of 8mm cine film and tape-recordings. This material could be broadly divided into a record of aspects of the area visited, and secondly, the

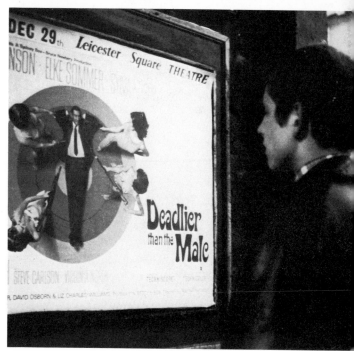

172

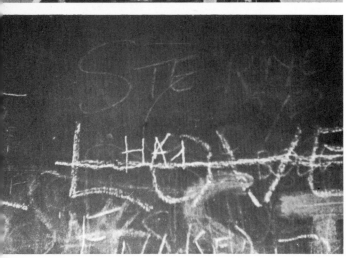

photographic evidence of human love being a fact of life in the dockland. At least six hours of playing time on tape was recorded. From this the group produced a booklet containing selections at some length from these tape-recordings, but it is only possible to print short extracts here:

WOMAN   We've been married twenty-five . . .

KELVIN   What do you think love is . . .?

WOMAN   I don't know . . . just a feeling between people that's all . . . (to husband) . . . Oh, they're joking . . . they've got to be!

ERICA   We're not, we're serious.

HUSBAND   They're not. They're taping it, aren't they? What do you want to know? You've got to give it thought, haven't you? I was in the navy when . . .

WOMAN   And he gave it a lot of thought there. (Laughs)

FIRST MAN   Yes. (Laughs) Well in my day we were taught not to make love to anybody whether we loved them or not, until we were married. You think this has gone, do you?

ANN   I think we rebel against it more now, but it's still drummed into us.

SECOND MAN   Do you think you should deprive the body of what it needs?

ANN   No. I can understand that people make love for the sake of making love but I don't think I'm one of those people.

SECOND MAN   I think you're just the same as anybody else, everybody's the same: everybody lies in bed and gets the same urges.

DAVID   Then your experience of love is a purely physical one?

MAN   No I've had psychological forms of love, too. What is love? Love is a state of maturity. It only comes with being with a person so many years that you've got such a bond you can't live without them.

DAVID   That's more 'dependence' than 'love', surely?

ANN   Is this love you feel for your Saviour a totally different sort of love you feel, say, for your husband or children?

SALVATION ARMY OFFICER   Yes, I think it is. Because He isn't a physical person and therefore you only love him because of what he's

173–175

done for you, what you're feeling inside, what's coming from him. Oh, this is horribly difficult, you obviously cannot love someone who is not physically here in the same way that you can love someone who is physically here.

ANN   You love the idea more than the . . .

SALVATION ARMY OFFICER   No, you experience God's love inside you. This is something you can experience.

FILM AND DRAMA

There are, in general, two approaches to drama activities in English schools; (either one is used to the exclusion of the other, or they co-exist or may be employed concurrently in a school). The one places a high value upon the training of the senses, regards acting as an art, and views the ultimate goal of all exercises and rehearsal as the production of a play. The other takes all dramatic activities as equal, regarding the main aim of performance at any time as an attempt to enrich the daily experience of living itself. The embodiment of this latter approach can be found in what is likely to be known to its participants as 'improvisation'. On the one hand a belief that the blood, sweat and tears of producing a play must prove the best means of developing pupils' abilities; on the other that simply to improvise, to play together rather than to produce a play, will provide opportunities of learning from each other. This kind of activity is considered by many teachers to be a valuable form of social education.

The camera, of course, can assist in attaining the ends sought by production or improvisation groups alike. In all staged performance there is an excitement for the performers that can be captured by the camera. Their pleasure, in fact, is communicable. But the vital question must be, 'What are the possible uses of the photographs after they have been taken?'

In some measure the answer has already been given earlier in the text. Story-making and script-writing by creating sequences of photographs have been mentioned, and, of course, the making of a film itself. Yet there are other possible functions for the camera within the drama class.

176–177

Gesture and action

For those studying acting techniques, the camera can become an invaluable aid. After the photographing of real or natural gesture, a profitable comparison for the actor can be made to the simulated or acted gestures of his fellows or himself before a mirror. The shades of expression of which the human face is capable, can be carefully documented with the camera (and later provide models when the making of stage masks is tackled). Attempts before the camera to translate words into actions by the actor can result in photographs that will prove for his benefit how successful or not his effort has been. In fact, the camera can be used by the actor in the street to produce documentary evidence of human behaviour on which his characterizations can be based.

The stage set

If the stage designer intends to base his set upon an actual structure, the process of photographing it may open his eyes to detail not apparent on inspection from a fixed angle. In looking through the view-finder of a camera he can exclude unwanted aspects of the scene, and the desired perspectives of the design can be discovered by using the camera.

The designer is often faced with the task of creating a sense of a particular location, real or imaginary, upon the school stage. This problem must always be a formidable one, but in terms of the school production it can become almost impossible, assuming the usual lack of money, materials, tools, working space and time. There can be considerable scope for experiment by the stage-craft department in creating a verisimilitude of place upon the stage by means of projecting images. Special projectors are required for filling large backdrops or cycloramas, but ingenious effects can be achieved by using ordinary cine or slide projectors. This form of stage decor can be effectively heightened by employing tape-recorders to project sound as an integral part of the set, rather than as a noises-off machine or a means of supplying music between the acts.

178–180

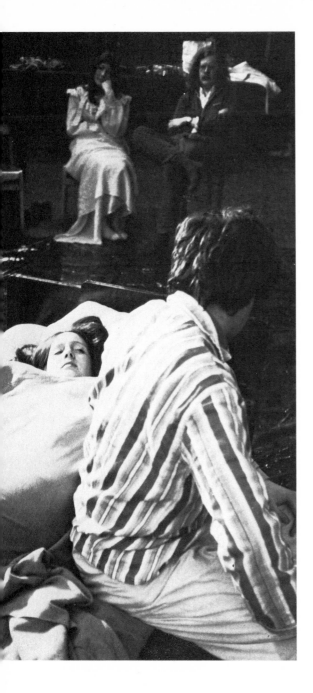

181 The improvisation group

The improvisation group and the camera

If an improvisation group wishes to return to subjects, or develop themes, a means of recording what takes place initially can help. With a record of what was actually said or done, dialogue can be resumed and action re-enacted later. In fact, the teacher may see the camera and tape-recorder as tools that can be used to shape an activity fundamentally without structure or direction into an end product. Thus, the photographs taken during one session might be discussed at the next and a development in terms of either a script or further improvised performance begun. The photographs shown here and on the following page, of young people wearing pyjamas and nightgowns remain as a token of an experience where improvisation was used to explore the force and pathos implicit in the act of sleeping around. The potency of the photograph in holding the attention of the group to the subject week by week is invaluable. The camera can be used to keep alive themes and topics that fade as verbal exposition and discussion dilutes them.

An introduction to the camera through handling it in group exercises has already been described. Increased familiarity with the camera will make possible its use on the stage within an improvised situation as it develops. The performing group must accept the fact that one of their number who is not occupying a central position in the action will take the photographs. When he is eventually drawn into the action of the improvised scene, the camera can be handed to another actor. Thus filming can proceed from succeeding angles as the scene unfolds. Each actor on stage is potentially a cameraman, and auxiliaries from off-stage can help, if needed.

Any group as it progresses has growing pains, but the direction of the growth will almost certainly be *inwards* as the members come to know and depend more fully upon one another. This is a natural process, but one that requires checking before it inhibits the outlook of its members. The group must seek ways and means to maintain a view of what is happening beyond their own sphere. Members of a drama group have their interest in performance itself to offer as a method of establishing contact with other people. One group, for example, decided to visit a monastery. Before the visit took place, they discussed their own motives for wanting to visit the monastery,

99

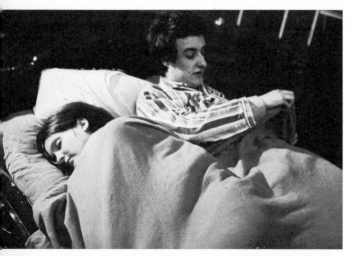

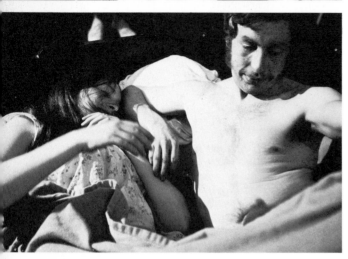

and also considered what uses could be made of both drama and film.

JUDY   Do we think of the people there, we say 'the monks', as individuals or a collective thing?

LYDIA   I thought a monk couldn't have a personality of his own, it's all channelled into one direction . . . .

DIANNE   Doesn't it amount to a form of escapism?

MICHAEL   Suppose you tell them you're an atheist?

DAVID   I have pictures of grey shadows walking about in their cloisters . . .

LYDIA   Don't we think we're like people going to a zoo, to see how they are different?

JUDY   We hope to find out their way of life and compare it to our own . . .

MICHAEL   We just hope to make contact with a different group of people . . .

LYDIA   We can only go prepared with ourselves.

The group's aim was to reach and make contact with their hosts, the Fathers, by using dramatic improvisation as a means of introducing themselves and their reasons for making the visit. They were keen to avoid being regarded as a travelling theatre unit or as visitors seeking a conducted tour of the monastery. It had been agreed before the journey that it would be better to meet people as people, and not as an audience to be played to, or as guides who would talk officially about their duties and the history, in this case, of the Carmelite Order. The group were committed to develop for themselves new terms by which to meet and negotiate with these people who were strangers to themselves and much older. Later, in the monastery, the members of the group used their form of dramatic improvisation to demonstrate the kind of people they were, and the abbot exhibited his sympathy and kindness by joining in. Both the photographs taken and the tape-recordings made remain as a record of this visit.

This same group find a continuing satisfaction in visiting other groups and using dramatic improvisation as a means of introducing themselves to their hosts. Both camera and tape-recorder fulfil a special function during these visits. They are used to record the event itself;

182–184   The improvisation group

but later, on the occasion of the next meeting, the photographs and tape-recordings are produced as evidence of the earlier link with the host or visiting group. Thus, a return to previous subjects can be made and a continuity in relationships maintained. Improvisations dealing with family problems are often staged by the group in mental hospitals in London, and in these situations the use of both camera and tape-recorder to capture aspects of problems as they emerge out of the performance by patients and members together has proved rewarding to all concerned, hospital staff, patients, and members of the group alike.

The opportunity certainly exists for all groups to explore the possibilities of drawing from the real world experiences recorded with the camera and tape-recorder that can be translated into a possibly new, and vital form of theatre.

FILM AND LITERATURE

Our principal concern is the possible uses the teacher may find for using filmstock in promoting the study of literature. The showing of the feature film and extract in support of the study of a particular work is a well established practice in most schools and colleges. But, can the camera and tape-recorder be used in the literature lesson to further a pupil's understanding of text and subject? The suggested exercises below might achieve this particular aim.

The use of the recording devices, cameras and tape-recorder, demand a subject. Film gravitates towards physical reality, and literature is a codification of human experience. What kind of subject material then exists to be recorded? Investigation should be regarded as the key activity. Any work being studied can be compared by investigation with a corresponding reality: the Lambeth of today as compared to the Lambeth described by Somerset Maugham; or, the temporary marooning of boys on a beach as compared to the predicament of the youngsters of Golding's *Lord of the Flies*.

From E M Forster's *A Passage to India* onwards can be traced a vast body of literature dealing with the issue of race conflict. An immigrant or Indian student might be called on to discuss the problems encountered by Aziz with a class, before the tape-recorder. The teacher, of course, may follow-up such exercises as he sees fit.

Most members of the public are likely to have been informed about any controversial aspect of

185 *Up the Junction*

a newly published book through the medium of television. Most will hold an opinion. The consulting of such opinions can prove useful to the literature class when discussing the book. If the book has earned a reputation, or notoriety, on publication it may be possible for the class to investigate subject or author.

The publishing of *Up the Junction,* by Nell Dunn, a collection of sketches of working class life in a London suburb, drew heavy criticism for its earthy qualities. Subsequently, it was adapted firstly for television, then the cinema, and the criticism renewed, even more heavily. But what were the feelings of the residents of the area about this matter? Could subjects described in the text be identified and recorded with the camera? One literature class undertook this project. Opinions recorded in the street were considerably varied:

> . . . I know the girl who done it very well. She only lived in Battersea a little while and what she has put in *Up the Junction* is nothing like it. I was born 'up the junction'. Porky, the flower seller, said it and she knows me very well . . .
> . . . I knew Nell Dunn when she lived here and there's no doubt she captured local colour, through close observation, and she met the people and lived with them and it was just factual, that's all there is about it . . .

and sometimes questions produced surprises. For example:

> Can we ask you a few questions about *Up the Junction*?
> No, afraid you can't. I don't live in the Junction. I know nothing about it at all.
> Have you been there?
> I was in the film. I am an actor. If you don't mind . . .

After spending the day in the area the group visited a West End cinema to see the feature *Up the Junction.* The material gathered finally was composed into a tape feature comprised of selected readings from the book, a synopsis of the film, statistical detail relating to abortion, early marriages, etc, and the tape-recorded interviews themselves.

This group had three productions to compare and discuss: book, television programme, and finally, a film feature. It could hardly be unrealistic to anticipate a stage version, with music. To what extent might future pupils come to regard a complex of book, film and television production, or possibly stage play as equal parts of a whole, a tripartite entity that emerges after the initial success of book, film or play? Will such a package deal enrich the lives of these pupils or confuse them? The teacher can easily test the liability of this event becoming a reality by asking his pupils to name their favourite stories. In the catalogue of *Filmed Books and Plays, 1928–1967* compiled by A G Enser, there are over 3,000 English language feature films listed without counting re-makes or any films made for television. It must be acknowledged that the existence of these films guarantees a chance for present day audiences of knowing texts that might have disappeared completely in an earlier time.

Collecting 'literature' with the tape-recorder
The tape-recorder can be used by groups of students and pupils in collecting samples of personal tastes in literature from members of the public in the street. To varying degrees, all people are walking anthologies of stories, poems and rhymes, and if the request for a sample is kindly

186   Patrick Anderson

made most human beings will try to oblige. The group of students who spent an afternoon in the streets of London talking to people about poetry and requesting them to offer samples of what they liked most, returned with a lot of material. Offers ranged from 'What's that one about the daffodils?' and, 'The only thing I can remember is the line *I wandered lonely as a cloud* which I hate', to the seven stanzas of a Victorian ballad offered by an old lady, and the young man who sang a love song to his own guitar accompaniment. After this experience, the students agreed that the compiling and printing of an anthology complete with photographs and illustrations of their own would prove an exciting project.

The writer as subject

If a class are asked, 'Where at this moment would you go if you wished to contact an author or poet?', its reactions may surprise the questioner. By many of the pupils or students the question will be regarded as irrelevant, 'Why bother with the author; it's his book we're concerned with.' Many might be astonished by the question, and it will be apparent that they hadn't really thought of authors existing in the flesh. Nevertheless, thousands of authors do exist, and some of these, at least, will be gratified by an interest expressed by students, to the extent of agreeing to meet the class itself (others will run for cover very quickly). If the characters or locations written about are inaccessible there remains the living author himself.

One group, asked 'to visit people who possess special skills . . . and wield an influence over large groups of people in the community' called by arrangement upon the writer, Patrick Andersson. Told '. . . your questions must be decided by yourselves . . .' the members carried out an exhaustive interview, gathering a great deal of information about the nature and business of authorship.

> . . . I remember the first poem that I wrote was a patriotic poem about England and it contained rhythm and it contained rhyme.—and it was absolutely God awful, no doubt. And I showed it to my favourite master and he said 'Doesn't scan old chap', and this, of course, put me off a bit.

187–190   The writer as subject

My mother . . . wanted me to go to a public school. And she said 'financially you have to get a scholarship or exhibition'. And I wasn't very good at Latin, and I was absolutely hopeless at maths, so she wrote to a number of headmasters, saying 'My son isn't much good at Latin or maths, but he's a poet . . .' And about 3 of the headmasters responded. The first was the headmaster of Lancing . . . I was summoned to the scholarship exam in London, when I was 13, and he said 'look during one of the exams I want you to write a poem'. The subject I chose was 'Speed' . . . I wrote a much too forceful, banal poem—I think the verses ended 'It's speed, speed, speed.' I wasn't too happy with it . . . He then interviewed me, and I must have been the most priggish small boy he'd ever met, because he said 'what are you reading?' And I said 'I've just finished Virginia Woolf's *Orlando*.'

Then, the headmaster of Sherborne (also one of those people conned by my mother) . . . and once again the same thing: 'During the Latin Verse exam I want you to write a poem . . . that's in two days' time . . . I want you to write about Sherborne Abbey . . . there it is . . . go and look at it . . . get the literature about it, do anything you like, but write the poem. . . . So I prepared this poem, and when I went into the exam, I think I wrote something like 85 lines in a fairly complicated semi-Spenserian stanzas in the two hours of the exam . . .'

Mr Anderson's hospitality was splendid, and later a much freer conversation took place within the bounds of the garden of the village pub. The idea of a working friendship between school or college and the writers and artists of the locality is worth promoting if their co-operation can be enlisted.

Using the camera as an aid in literature study

The author's use of language can be examined by the group, together, using the camera to record physical attempts to demonstrate meaning. Thus: *'The devil!' exclaimed Ferguson with quiet chagrin.*

What possibly does 'quiet chagrin' look like? Attempts by the members of the group to express this, not in words, but by facial gesture can be recorded by the camera. Again: 'She gave me a keen look' can prove more challenging than might be expected. 'What,' your students might be asked, 'is the difference between *a keen look* and *a pointed stare?*' An involvement in performance of this kind can be useful in elucidating the meaning of particular expressions used by an author. Such exercises can engage students in the investigation of the differences that exist between physical gestures that declare human emotion. The writer struggles hard to describe such gestures, depending upon such description to delineate character.

Extracting the essence

While discussing a novel or story it is useful to ask the student to imagine he is a photographer who has been called *into* the story at some point, and ask him to describe the scene. If he chooses a climatic moment in the story, his task might be to produce a sequence of still photographs that capture the essence of the event. In practice, the student should choose the moment of narrative to be visualized and create the scene with the help of actors, perhaps his classmates. He should photograph it carefully with a determination that his pictures will reveal all important detail. Thus, such a well known story as *An Odour of Chrysanthemums* by D H Lawrence contains a scene in which the miner's wife awaits her husband's return from the pit. He is late, and her anxiety grows, but it is compounded with other feelings of resentment and anger. A student's attempt to produce a sequence of photographs that would illustrate the flux of the woman's emotions during her vigil should exercise his understanding of this character's behaviour. The miner is killed and finally laid out in the parlour of their cottage. His wife places some chrysanthemums by his body. These are the kind of flowers he gave her on their wedding day. The obvious pathos of this scene might be photographed and linked to the text by any student prepared to tackle such an unmitigatedly sentimental passage. Finally, these exercises can be displayed to all studying this particular story.

Literature versus living

The principal purpose of the projects outlined above is to establish that the spheres and levels of living described in literature will have parallels in the world of the reader. If he chooses he can look for those parallels. It is unfortunate how often within the still centres of the examination forms of high schools and colleges, literature is studied in depth, without an acknowledgment that the story, play or poem being discussed was produced out of an experience of the author within the compass of the real world. Any danger that literature might become a minor branch of study is a saddening prospect, because potentially it is a useful aid to living for all human beings. It is an index of possible experiences, thoughts and actions that assists people who strive to make purposeful decisions in their lives. There is too great a risk of the teacher himself using literature as an aid in teaching the English language, and not treating it as a subject itself.

5　Working space

Throughout this book it has been assumed that the teacher interested in film work is likely to lack the working spaces, film-stage, sound studio and editing room, that would best enable him to organise a full programme of activities. A further assumption has been made that he is likely to struggle in cramped surroundings to use such activity methods in his teaching as those described earlier, while more fortunate associates have the use of science laboratories, gymnasia, craft and art rooms, and even language laboratories. The existence of these, of course, signifies the authorities' acceptance of the need for the teaching of the subjects they serve. However, what kind of facilities does the film teacher really need?

Above all else in his room, he will require a flexibility of fittings and equipment that can be easily manoeuvred. He will be served best by a room which possesses a floor, walls, and ceiling that can be used for mounting displays, and windows, or at least artificial light sources, which ensure the brightest lighting possible.

He will not require the heavy-weight paraphernalia of the old-style classroom, the teacher's desk or the blackboard that folds or runs on a trolley; and he will be greatly obstructed by a superabundance of desks (the best means ever found of shackling a superabundance of children) that can only be moved or stacked in a corner with difficulty. He will find it difficult to work in a room with a door that cannot be opened as easily from the inside as the outside. He will need to regard *outside* as merely an extension of *inside* and vice versa.

It seems important that a serious re-thinking of the function of that basic unit of the school building, the class-room, be carried out. Apart from any demand to be made for the accommodation of new subjects, it should be recognised that most class-rooms are cramping and restricting areas in which to work for most pupils and teachers. It is the usual policy that the class-room is not to be left without permission, and the parent is rarely welcome to visit other than on Open Days. (Other institutions such as hospitals and prisons hold similar events.) There can be an unhealthy sense of a pupil's schooldays being of necessity a period of quarantine, during which he is to be protected as much as possible from the germ-ridden environment in which, nevertheless, he lives when out of school. In effect, the suggestions given above contain a proposal that the present working areas known as *class-rooms* be stripped in order that teachers can build activity-based programmes from ground level. The business of film-making, display and English drama exercises cannot be easily or very successfully carried out in a room full of desks. Neither can visitors be catered for properly in this kind of workroom. Can a legitimate case be made for the removal of the desks? Schools certainly might consider the creating of rooms reserved for those pupils who have been set a writing task by the teacher. In any eventuality, it remains possible to believe that fine writing might be done on knee or improvised support if the set task is happily received by your pupils and your command is their wish.

Going out into the street with camera and tape-recorder should guarantee a return with collected sound and image sequences. While the experience of gathering these might be viewed as a major part of the exercise, their consequent development and use is really of equal importance. Ordinarily, such material is too interesting or entertaining to leave on the shelf, and there are many possible methods of presenting these findings to other groups. You may invite visitors to your room as an audience, or choose to grant them Guest Pupil status, to be involved, when the pupils wish, in any of the work in progress. Whatever your choice, it will be necessary to plan your activities-room programme carefully.

A BASIC UNIT

Many teachers will ask, 'what exactly do I need to equip this unit?' Of course, any answer must consider the subject and programme envisaged.

191 The workshop

Nevertheless, whatever items are desired, it should be realised that only one room is likely to be made available by the school, and, in fact, it is desirable that all the activities planned take place in the room, that it become known and talked about as *a centre*.

The equipment bought should be chosen for its toughness and manoeuvrability. It will have to be tough to withstand constant handling. (It should not be overlooked that the group given an abundance of sophisticated equipment with which to work often becomes confused and suffers an embarrassment of riches.)

a Cameras: as many standard and super 8mm cameras as can be owned, or even borrowed. The same condition applies to still cameras
b 8mm camera with zoom lens for animation, stills titling, etc
c Single lens reflex camera for taking slides
d A set of photofloods and several quartz-iodine lamps
e A tripod
f A supply of extension cables
g An 8mm sound (magnetic) projector

h Editing equipment: at least four editors (film viewers) and splicers
i Two mains (permanently installed, working off main power supply) tape-recorders, mounted on trolleys if possible
j Portable tape-recorders for fieldwork: as with cameras, as many as can be mustered by buying or borrowing
k Tape-recorder leads for transfer of recordings from portable machine to mains (non-portable) recorder (master tape)
l Two tape-splicers
m Slide projector, preferably of the automatic kind
n *Concept* or *loop* projector for display viewing of 8mm loops made from film shot by pupils
o A record player

Some rostra, folding screens, and at least two baby spot lights will assist when a display is intended. Obviously storage may be a problem, and cupboards are therefore necessary, unless an area outside the studio can be utilized. If a teacher decides to place the onus on each group he teaches to promote their own projects, it will be necessary to be able to clear the room as quickly as possible. The following account of one group's workshop is an example of presentation of films and drama exercises to visitors designed to simplify contact with them and allow for stimulating criticism and helpful suggestions.

The hall was approximately 24m by 15m, lit by neon lighting and in good overall condition. Our first step was to clear the hall of all furniture and introduce twelve trestle tables for use by our members as work benches. These were placed close to the centre sections of the two longer walls and two chairs placed behind each. This left both ends of the hall clear for other uses. Care was taken to leave the centre area of the hall free for drama performance. Each bench was clearly labelled by the users with their names and project titles. Apart from the seating provided for the members of the group, the only other seating available anywhere in the hall was where a semi-circle of chairs 'sealed off' an area known to us as the *Rehearsal Corner*. This was used during our *bench work* periods as an area in which members could display improvisation exercises to visitors. At the opposite end we placed our 8mm and 16mm editing equipment; sound amplification unit; film projectors and general supplies of materials. Our members took or borrowed whatever they needed from this supply point: portable tape-recorders, typewriters, art materials, etc. It was expected that the demonstrations of the technical processes of filming would fill a substantial part of each two hour programme. But it was hoped that on a given signal a rapid transition could be made from the mechanics of film-making to the group activity of improvised drama. It was felt to be important not to allow our visitors to be swept aside by the re-organisation of our seating arrangements. Therefore they had not been provided with seats at the benches, and when the moment came when we wished our visitors to join us in a seated circle, chairs were quickly introduced into the hall by a duty crew especially appointed to make this change swiftly and smoothly. This system worked satisfactorily, and we found that all our visitors were speedily drawn together with our members.

This group made direct invitation to the public to join them during this working period. In their letter addressed to all they stated, 'A workshop presentation, we believe, allows all responsible to show their work and share it with an audience'. Could such an event have a regular place during the normal timetable of a school? What value might there be for teacher and pupils if the public were to be considered as a vital agency to be referred to for opinion and advice in the course of any teaching day? The idea needed to be explored. Obviously many teachers (especially headmasters) will shrink at the thought of an unsanctioned flow of adults into their domain, but the prospect of such action requires a cool, unhysterical look.

What will happen to class teaching? To be deprived of the straight-jacket accessories of desks and the dictatorial use of 'take out your pens and write' means that you are compelled to deal with the interests of your pupils more directly. Many teachers will demand recognition for the values of the formal lesson. It is for each individual English teacher himself to decide how formal he wishes his lessons to be. Once a room is empty, however, the teacher who wishes to give the more traditional form of lesson will find returning the chairs and desks altogether too time-consuming. He cannot indulge in half measures and has to be committed either to the old style formation, or accept that a number of chairs must suffice and that pupils will write on their knees or elsewhere, library or writing room. The following quotation is from an account by an English teacher who chose to use drama as a basis for almost all of his English teaching.

After several consultations I had word that the desks could be removed, and any written work was to be done on temporary desks, tables and chairs of the folding kind, easily moved in and out of the room. A store of these was eventually obtained from the school canteen. But before these alterations took place I was able to arrange the desks in a circle and try *arena* teaching. The lecturing position with your class *en bloc* before you was disposed of and a point beside any member of the group, seated in a desk, served instead. The circle brought a less didactic, more conversational tone to many of my lessons. There was also the advantage of being able to call any boy from

194

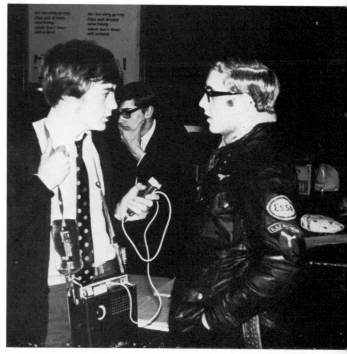

195

196

The removal of my classroom's paraphernalia left it bare and invited development in a new direction. Many boys anticipated that it was acquiring an extra significance to being a classroom. Their talk indicated that there was scope for a wide variety of *social functions*.

The result for this particular teacher was a growth outside his class-room teaching of an interest in other activities. The room eventually acquired a coffee bar made by the children, and a small proscenium stage was constructed:

As I was struggling to deal with the problem of the school's lack of equipment and space, I was attracted to the idea of creating a small theatre which could be self-contained and not too demanding when it came to finding sufficient materials for settings. A little theatre in which presentation would be scaled to conserve both time and money and of dimensions to accommodate the child as performer, scene-builder and producer. In any setting here, the proximity of the performer to audience would demand sincere, fluent performance and children, at best, can be relied upon to become sincerely involved in any performance they may give. Simply staged, vivid production was my aim.

Apart from establishing a method of drama production that eliminated the lengthy procedures of term-long rehearsal, the room became a centre where interesting lessons could be developed further and repeated or staged for other classes. The removal of the desks had created a space that could be filled with visitors.

The room described above was situated in a secondary modern school, attended by eleven to sixteen-year-olds, in an old army hut that had served for a classroom since the end of World War Two. It seems quite sensible that such a utility building should have been made available for this experiment. Standing at some distance from the main body of the school it was easier to regard it as possessing an individual identity; a sense of being *a place*. The main road was close by and visitors, mainly ex-pupils, were frequent visitors. For the teacher wishing to experiment with the mobile classroom which can be situated outside the school, it should be advisable to consider the whole range of accommodation available to the traveller, tents, caravans, and

his seat and quickly involve him, where possible, in a demonstration to support any theory he advanced. It might be a simple showing of how he had caught a fish, or the miming of a word, verb or adjective. Yet if he was obliged to match his words to gesture, frequently a clearer, more forceful expression of ideas resulted. The distractions were, I believe, fewer than they might have been in other class-rooms of the school. We gave our undivided attention to our own opinions and actions. We had an uncluttered space in which to work, to start activities that might be eventually concluded at a desk or easel, but which for us began dynamically on the floor, moving, feeling and thinking spontaneously. Within the compass of our limited resources, words had to become *things—a spade* became albeit an improvised spade; and such words as *city* or *grief* could be nothing but the sum total of every member of the group's understanding of them translated into action and feeling, and then reconsidered by the group in the light of all heard and seen.

lorries. It seems likely that many educational uses might be found for the travelling classroom or *workshop*.

METHODS OF PRESENTATION AND PROGRAMME PLANNING

The pupil who has produced a sequence of photographs must wish to know who is to see them and how they might be displayed. Did the group who made the documentary film about immigrant children make it primarily to prove themselves to be film-makers or was it made with an audience in mind? The dramatic improvisation may prove so absorbing that the participants wish to develop it into a play they can perform to an audience. The poetry written by the class is exciting, could it be read to an audience, or printed and distributed? Thus, the teacher faces the problem of organizing programmes of work for the groups under his direction, and must advise them upon the best possible means of presenting their work.

A special emphasis should be placed on the importance of planning ahead and preparing for the extra demands that will certainly occur when a class divides into smaller groups to work on projects. The teacher must be prepared to meet the requests of pupils for the equipment they need, as they make them, if their projects are to proceed smoothly and be completed on time. There is an enormous advantage in having a work centre. The would-be film-maker can waste as much time as he uses to profit if he is obliged to resort to separate rooms to carry out different tasks. Any time spent in carrying equipment between rooms is wasted time. Also, if the equipment is heavy, and it often is, back strain for the carrier may result, or the machines may be damaged in the moving. But the greatest risk of a film or play *not* being completed before the end of a school term lies in insufficient planning. It is not enough to have the equipment and know how to use it; the studio planning is vitally important and must incorporate every detail from bookings to insurance coverage for the portable equipment used in the street.

THE EMPTY SPACE

The class that can be offered an empty room in

which to mount their *presentation* should be able to consider all possible combinations of effects to be achieved by means of using display, film projection and drama. If the walls, floor and ceiling are as free as possible from encumbrances, they are available as *a* display panels to be used as mounting bases or painted *b* as neutral settings for film work and drama *c* potentially as light reflectors, having a light-coloured, polished surface. Any use of standard formulae for the displaying of work is entirely the right of the group, but there should be excellent opportunities to encourage experiments by group members.

POSSIBLE PROJECTS

Much teaching can take place within this studio that can be directly related to the course work that is devoted to helping students pass examinations. Outside the school in the larger world of the community lies the opportunity for the teacher to promote a form of social studies or English that is not examinable (and thus often deemed, quite erroneously, unnecessary for examination classes) but of vital importance. These studies should be concerned with the students discovering how community problems arise, how they were or might be solved and what personal parts they have to play themselves in these community matters. Obviously, these studies will be social inasmuch as they focus upon community affairs and life; they' will be concerned with language insofar as purposive talking in the street or with official spokesmen occurs and specialized uses of language are employed. Two programmes are outlined; the first was entirely studio-based and related to pupils' studies:

How might the teacher bring his students to a wider perspective of literature when he is committed to a syllabus representing only a small part of the body of world literature? Furthermore, what amount of time can the teacher hope to find to discuss the novel or poetry or play as a creative act in comparison to other acts of creation, other art forms? These questions were considered to be of importance and accordingly a supplementary programme was devised to be carried out in a workshop which allowed the students to focus their attention upon aspects of the modern art movements of today and yesterday. Extracts from this carefully prepared programme should illustrate the form of the activities undertaken by the students:

Week 2 The Short Story
Crystallisation
Maxims, proverbs, aphorisms, parables, fables, Buddhist stories, jokes, the bar-room story, the 'short story' poem (duplicated material prepared and distributed)
Toothache Frank Sargeson
Exercise 'To paraphrase with pith and poignancy' an exercise with cut-out pictures and words

After discussing examples of the above, word and image statements upon the theme of *Time* were completed.

Week 3 The Short Story
Reading of *The Alcoholic Veteran with the Washboard Cranium* Henry Miller
Exercise The writing of a short story with the help of the tape-recorder

After reading an extract from this story together in class, each student was asked to record a conversation held with a person outside the college, and finally, after transcribing the recording, to incorporate this into the writing of a short story.

Week 9 *Eating*

The compilation of an anthology of descriptions of meals and eating taken from literature, followed by the filming of a meal, pre-cooked, and eaten in the studio. Several travel posters, tablecloths and some cutlery serving as décor in the corner of the studio representing a café.

Week 11 Desert Islands
An anthology of extracts from novels dealing with the above theme (Printed material distributed)
What would you do if marooned on a desert island? A group improvisation

Such a theme, frequently used by writers, led to discussion of the parallel theme of *isolation*. The group improvisation was launched by drawing a chalk circle around the students, declaring the inner area an island, and discussing survival prospects from that position.
A flexibility and fluency of action became

possible in these exercises because there was sufficient space in which to implement them quickly. The printing and distribution of a programme to the students at the beginning of the course prepared them for and, to some extent, helped to involve them in, the event before it occurred. Feature films, extracts and films made by students were included in this programme.

Viridiana (extract)	*Director* Luis Bunuel
La Jetée	*Director* Chris Marker
Robinson Crusoe	*Director* Luis Bunuel

112

All the above exercises were studio-based and intended essentially for the students' own sake. By way of contrast, the second project was based on looking for an answer to the questions: 'What is it really like to live in this community?' and 'How does it differ from my way of life?' This had an outward direction, and the inevitable and desired result for each student was a personal commitment to a geographic area for a sustained period of time. The location was Stratford in East London, and the project was carried out by a group of trainee child care nurses. For each week throughout a six-month period, they visited the area, equipped with cameras and tape-recorders. The cameras were used to record all aspects of the experience: their visits to schools, factories, local government offices, etc. Tape-recorders were used to record all their conversations with residents of the area, and other official figures who agreed to be interviewed by the girls. Contact with these local government officers was usually made by letter, but probably the most satisfying contacts came by a continuing association with

the people encountered in public places; cafés became the ideal meeting places.

Meanwhile, all information gathered was displayed in the college workshop and supplemented weekly. Printed material found in the area was carried back and either exhibited intact, or through the medium of a wall collage. Successful recordings were transferred to a master tape or printed for use as study material. Stills were enlarged and displayed. 8mm film was edited and used as study material by social studies groups.

A systematic enquiry was carried out into the different aspects of the life of this community. Housing, schools, care of the mentally sick, were examined and a statistical analysis attempted. Personal attitudes of local inhabitants to religion, marriage, etc were also investigated. An attempt was made to ensure that each student became as familiar with Stratford as possible, to avoid the risk of making snap judgements based upon a cursory tour of the area.

197–198   Project on Stratford, East London

199–201 Project on Stratford, East London

Film was used as an aid and only as an aid; aesthetic considerations were never more than of secondary significance. An understanding of subject was the paramount aim. But it was recognised later, unfortunately, that the resulting display of findings within the college, some ten miles from the area, offered little to residents of Stratford. The college was altogether too far away and too intimidating an institution for the residents of Stratford to visit. With hindsight, it can now be seen that the group would have been better advised to stage their presentation of their findings within the community, in borrowed accommodation if possible, perhaps the church hall or public library. If the group had given more thought to audience they might have resolved to make and show the film as a useful contribution to the welfare of the community.

It is obvious that filmstock may be regarded as a teaching material to be used for many different purposes inside and outside of the classroom. But regardless of how it is used, the production of photograph or screen image always poses the same question: 'For whose benefit have these images been produced?' It is unsatisfactory to say that the film-maker can work for himself alone, screen art is nothing if not a mass medium, and every film is an effort on the part of the maker to express his views or feelings to other human beings.

Yet, in school and college film-making, the accent is so often placed upon the need to learn how to make a film without any questioning of who its potential audience might be. To take it for granted that the audience will be teachers and parents, seems both a limited teaching aim and a limiting goal to set pupils. It is exciting to concentrate upon pleasing, stirring or provoking the sensibilities of a real audience, to work with a hope of a return of interest, and a continuing contact after the act. To ask a group making a film to define the audience they wish to reach is also to demand that clear and careful thought be given to the shape, substance, and meaning of the enterprise. It certainly means that the film will be made with human beings, an audience, in mind rather than as an exercise in the practice of camera technique. The obvious question that follows is, 'What kind of films can school film-makers hope to produce that will provide a service, entertainment or information, to other groups of people?' There seems no reason why a school with its own film unit cannot produce its own teaching-aid films while learning about *the subject* in the making. Equally, there can be no adequate reason for not undertaking the making of documentary films about aspects of the community the school stands as part of, to be used by agencies of that area. These can serve as records of change as time progresses. Film-making can be profitably employed by those teachers who would wish to ascertain what more positive role the school might fill in the community life. Inasmuch as the community is taxed to pay for materials used in the school, it is well worth considering a policy of re-investment of those materials in order to acquire more. Any school or college is in a position to attempt this, by making a film definitely *aimed at a public audience*. Its drawing power, it should be noted, is likely to depend much more upon choice of subject and good publicity than upon guaranteeing the audience a demonstration of film-making expertise.

The film made by the individual, described earlier as the personal film, presents a different problem to the teacher in his role of producer. It is doubtful whether this kind of film-maker can accept the idea of a tangible audience. Usually such a film-maker wishes, quite legitimately, to address his films to a universal audience, to anyone who will claim to understand them.

Again, the teacher must recognise that the making of this kind of film, in fact, any form of solo production, will probably result in the maker wishing to possess his own work. This is a reasonable desire, particularly as films made in schools are rarely finished in the time allotted on the timetable, and the film-maker is likely to have laboured as much in his own time as in school hours. Thus, the teacher must settle the issue of eventual ownership.

Each teacher according to his pupils' abilities and needs must decide what kind of programme might be attempted. But a basic need for an allocation of tape-recorders and film equipment will exist and a reasonable supply of basic materials, chiefly filmstock and magnetic sound tape, is necessary. However, it is particularly important that the teacher should be aware that the provision of equipment is not the most important step to be taken in establishing film-making in his school, but only the first.

To have solved the problem of housing this form of combined operations from the beginning means that the teacher controlling these lessons will find his task made considerably easier. The empty room may seem to any outside the teaching profession a very simple request. But apart from real lack of space existing in most schools and colleges there is another possible and all too familiar reason for its non-availability on request. This, simply said, is fear of experiment. But surely in every school, in some corner, a certain degree of experimentation can be justified? The inhibiting contours of the formal classroom must change, and are changing at the infant and junior (elementary school) level of education. Desks have their uses, but a desk-bound education is

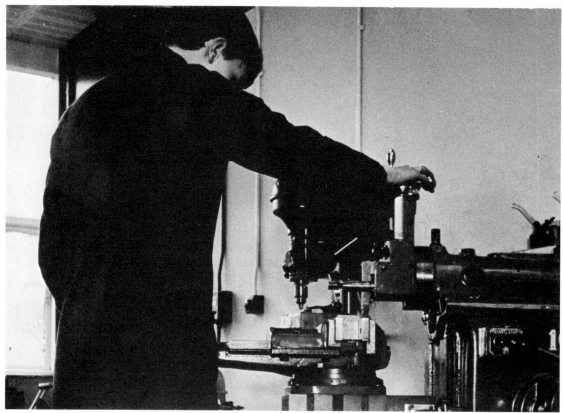

202 The Lathe. An instructional film made by the students of a college of further education for engineering students within the establishment

necessarily a limited one, from every point of view.

In any school or college there is a need to promote a sense of community within a community among pupils or students and staff. Most schools strive to do this, but unfortunately, more often than not, consider that a separation is necessary between the daily labour of class studies and what a film, art, drama, debating or any other society attempts to achieve. Any school or college in setting up a workshop should be able to establish a mobilisation of the arts subjects, at least, in such a way that will mean they will be more realistically applied to dealing with the problems of communication between human beings.

116

Any created space opens up the prospect of changing methods and changing relationships

203 and 204   Floor space provides a valuable working area—all too frequently neglected—for individual or group discussion

205 and 206   Floor squared with masking tape in preparation for concerted group movement to tape-recorded sound 'concrete'

Eating can nourish the body *and* the mind

20/ and 208   Filmed 'eating spectacle' by art students

Changing your *own* image in school is exciting . . .

209 and 210   Exercise involving juniors in drawing round their own bodies and painting the cut-outs as they choose

for both teacher . . .   and his pupils

211   Teacher filmed by junior pupils   212   Clown project carried out by juniors

118

The playground or school yard offers scope for messier, noiser, action-packed ventures

213 Large-scale painting project with secondary
school children

214   Film making with secondary school boys

But there will always be more working space outside rather than inside any school or college

215   Drama and film exercise in an adventure playground

Film libraries which supply films and extracts
British Film Institute
42/43 Lower Marsh, London SE1
Central Booking Agency
102 Dean Street, London W1
Concord Films Council
Nacton, Ipswich, Suffolk
Connoisseur Films Ltd
16mm Film Library, 58 Wardour Street,
London W1
Contemporary Film Ltd
14 Soho Square, London W1
Modern Talking Picture Service (industrials)
1212 Avenue of the Americas, New York, NY
Cinema 16 (theatricals)
120 East 34 Street, New York, NY
McGraw-Hill (educational)
330 West 42 Street, New York, NY
United World Films (educational)
221 Park Avenue South, New York, NY

Commercially-sponsored free-loan films
Rank Film Library
1 Aintree Road, Perivale, Middlesex
Shell-mex Ltd
Shell Centre, London SE1
BP Co Ltd
Brittanic House, Moor Lane, London EC2
British Transport Films
Melbury House, Melbury Terrace, London NW1

Free-loan films can often be borrowed from embassies and national agencies.

Stills and cine equipment
Johnsons of Hendon Ltd
Hendon Way, London NW4
Wallace Heaton
Bond Street, London W1
Pelling and Cross Ltd
Baker Street, London W1

For all requests and complete **catalogs** *contact:*
F & B Ceco
315 West 43 Street, New York, NY 10036

Burns and Sawyer Cine Equipment Co
6424 Santa Monica Blvd, Los Angeles, California 90038

In addition **editing equipment** is available from

Acmade Works
Colneside Works, Oxford Road, Denham, Bucks
R. Rigby Premier Works
Northington Street, Gray's Inn Road, London WC1
Photographic Electrical
71 Dean Street, London W1

Laboratories for film processing
Brent Laboratories
North Circular Road, Cricklewood, London NW2
Humphries and Co Ltd
71–81 Whitfield Street, London W1
Kay Laboratories Ltd
49a Oxford Road, Finsbury Park, London N4
Movielab
619 West 54 Street, New York, NY 10019
DuArt
245 West 55 Street, New York, NY 10019
General Film Laboratory
1546 North Argyle Avenue, Hollywood, California 90028

Sound transfer and dubbing
Audio Systems
68 Harrowdene Road, Wembley, Middlesex
Manhattan Audio Co
460 West 54 Street, New York, NY
Telesound
6296 Melrose, Hollywood, California 90038

Stripping film, 8mm and 16mm
RCA Film Services
Heron Trading Estate, Westfields Road, Acton, London W3

Tape-recorders
Ferrograph
Vortexion
Truvox
Uher (available through *Martel Electronic Sales*
1199 Broadway, New York, NY)
Obtainable from the manufacturer when ordered
by an educational establishment

Second-hand equipment
F & B Ceco and *Burns and Sawyer*

Outdated stocks of photographic paper, film and
second-hand equipment can be obtained through
Harringay Photographic Suppliers
435 Green Lanes, London N4

In the USA local production companies or TV
stations often have outdated stock they are
pleased to sell at reduced prices or give away.

The most useful range of books upon technical aspects of film-making for the teacher are published by the Focal Press and the Fountain Press. Both produce relatively cheap handbook series covering most aspects of cine and still photography. I have found the following Focal Press books particularly helpful:

The Technique of Documentary Film Production W Hugh Baddeley (1969) (Hastings House New York, 1963)
The Technique of Film Animation John Halas and Roger Manvell (1969) (Hastings House New York 1968)
The Technique of Film Editing Karel Reisz and Gavin Millar (1970) (Hastings House New York 1967)
The Technique of Special Effects Cinematography Raymond Fielding (1971) (Hastings House New York 1965)

The Fountain Press publications give extremely lucid descriptions of how to deal with interior and outdoor lighting problems.

Exposing Cine Film Brian Gibson (1960)
Lighting for Cine Brian Gibson (1962)

Photography and film-making magazines should not be neglected. These contain a great deal of technical advice, and, particularly, discussions of the merits and demerits of equipment that has recently appeared on the market. They do tend, however, to treat any freewheeling approach to film use with suspicion. The best known, *Amateur Photographer,* is a weekly magazine, and *Film-making* is published monthly. *Creative Camera,* published monthly, is always an exciting visual treat, and worth buying for inspiration's sake.

Studio Vista publish an interesting range of books upon film-making. The following four should prove useful to the teacher:

A–Z of Movie-making Wolf Rilla (1970) (Viking Press New York 1970)

Animated Film-making Anthony Kinsey (1970)
How to Make Animated Movies (Viking Press New York 1970)
Group Film-making Robert Ferguson (1969) (Viking Press New York 1970)
The Underground Film Sheldon Renan (1968)
An Introduction to the American Underground Film (E P Dutton New York 1967)

Studio Vista also publish a series of handbooks dealing with visual media. The undermentioned book is an extremely well illustrated description of the making of films from paintings, still photographs and all kinds of graphic forms.

Grafilm J Bryne-Daniel (1970) (Van Nostrand Reinhold New York 1970)

Tantivy Press have recently launched a *Screen Textbooks* series, and the most useful to the teacher is likely to be:

Practical Motion Picture Photography Russell Campbell, editor (A Zwemmer Ltd 1971) (A S Barnes New Jersey 1970)

The British Film Institute offer the teacher:

Film-making in Schools and Colleges Edited by Peter Harcourt and Peter Theobald (1966)
This is a useful compendium of personal approaches to film-making within the school time-table.

Yet, apart from the technical data available as mentioned above, perhaps a more inspiring source of information is to be found in the essays and autobiographical accounts written by film-makers describing the making of their films. The following books contain vivid accounts of the actual process of filming by the film-makers themselves:

The Camera and I Joris Ivens (International Publishers New York 1970)

Film-makers on Film-making Edited by Harry R Geduld (Pelican 1970) (Indiana University Press 1969)

Hollywood Cameramen Charles Higham (Thames and Hudson 1970) (Indiana University Press 1970)

How It Happened Here Kevin Brownlow (Secker and Warburg London 1968) (Doubleday New York, 1968)

Losey on Losey Joseph Losey and Tom Milne (Secker and Warburg 1967) (Doubleday New York 1968)

The New American Cinema Gregory Battcock editor (E P Dutton New York 1967)

Recommended books for general reading

An Introduction to the Art of the Movies Lewis Jacobs (Noonday Press New York 1960)

CSE Examinations in Film Roger Watkins (British Film Institute 1969)

Film: An Anthology Daniel Talbot (University of California Press 1969)

Film as Art Rudolf Arnheim (University of California Press 1957) (Faber and Faber London 1958)

The Film Experience Roy Huss and Norman Silverstein (Dell Publishing Company New York 1969)

The Film Sense Sergei Eisenstein (Faber and Faber London 1968) (Harcourt Brace Jovanovitch New York 1969)

Film Teaching Stuart Hall Roy Knight Albert Hunt Alan Lovell (British Film Institute 1968)

Film World: A Guide to Cinema Ivor Montagu (Pelican 1964)

Grierson on Documentary edited by Forsyth Hardy (Harcourt-Brace and Company New York 1946) (revised edition Faber and Faber London 1966)

The Innocent Eye: The Life of Robert J Flaherty (W H Allen London 1963) (Harcourt-Brace and Company New York 1966)

King Cohn Bob Thomas (Putnam New York 1967) (Barrie and Rockliff London 1967)

Talking About the Cinema Jim Kitses with Ann Mercer (British Film Institute 1966)

Teaching About the Film J M L Peters (UNESCO Paris 1961)

Theory of Film Siegfried Kracauer (Oxford University Press 1965)

US and Canadian photography and film magazines

Alphabetical Guide to Motion Picture, Television, and Video Tape Productions
American Cinematographer
Animated Film Concepts
Cinema
Film Culture
Film Quarterly
Film Maker
Industrial Photography
International (German)
Leica Photography
Moving Image
Photo Kina
Photo Methods for Industry
Photo Technique
Take One (Canadian)

Supersound Electronic Products
114 Mount Pleasant Road, Hastings, Sussex
Cine Magnetics
529 North Barry Avenue, Mamaroneck, New York 10543

Note to US readers

Although local libraries do not generally rent films to school groups, most state libraries and state universities do. The film department of your local library is, however, a source of catalogs and film reference books.

Films can be rented directly from the major national film distributors (such as M-G-M, Columbia/Screen Gems, Paramount, Janus), and they will send you their catalogs upon request.

A complete listing of film companies and distributors, and a listing of available feature films, is included in the comprehensive *Directory of 8mm and 16mm Films Available for Rental, Sale and Lease in the United States* (Educational Film Library Association, Inc, New York). This directory costs $7.50 and can be obtained by writing to: Continental 16, Book Order Department, 241 East 34th Street, New York, N Y.

A catalog of the films is available on request from The Museum of Modern Art. Application should be made to: Circulation Director, Department of Film, The Museum of Modern Art, 11 West 53rd Street, New York, N Y.

Index

125